SMOKING NOT ALLOWED

GILDA BERGER

SMOKING NOT ALLOWED

THE DEBATE

FRANKLIN WATTS

LONDON | NEW YORK | TORONTO | SYDNEY | 1987

Photographs and cartoons courtesy of: Photo Researchers, Inc.: pp. 2
(Joseph Szabo), 16 (Arthur Tress), 92 (Melissa Hayes English), 99
(Peter G. Aitken), 120 (Top—Kenneth Murray), 127 (Getsug / Anderson);
Rothco Cartoons: pp. 10 and 80 (Gary Huck); The Bettmann Archive,
Inc.: pp. 23, 45, 54, 105 (top); New York Public Library Picture
Collection: pp. 31, 36, 41, 63, 104, 105 (bottom); American Cancer
Society: pp. 70, 75; USDA Photo: p. 120 (bottom—Sam Case).

Library of Congress Cataloging-in-Publication Data

Berger, Gilda.
Smoking not allowed.

Includes bibliographies and index.
Summary: Discusses the legal, economic, civil
rights, and health issues surrounding the debate
over legislation governing smoking.
1. Tobacco habit—United States—Juvenile
literature.   2. Tobacco—Physiological effect—Juvenile
literature.   3. Smoking—Law and legislation—United
States—Juvenile literature.   [1. Smoking.
2. Smoking—Law and legislation]   I. Title.
HV5760.B47   1987   362.2'9   87-10575
ISBN 0-531-10420-6

CONTENTS

SMOKING NOT ALLOWED

PART I
BACKGROUND

WHATEVER HARM WE DO, PLEASE REMEMBER A LOT OF JOBS DEPEND ON US...
TOBACCO INDUSTRY

ROTHCO
huck '81
DOCTORS · CLERGY · UNDERTAKERS · STONECUTTERS · GRAVE DIGGERS

ONE

A FOUR-HUNDRED-YEAR-OLD CONTROVERSY

"Smoking Not Allowed" signs are going up everywhere —in offices and factories, in planes and trains, in restaurants and waiting rooms, in libraries and museums, in movie theaters and sports arenas, in boutiques and department stores. Smokers, says U.S. Surgeon General C. Everett Koop, will increasingly be segregated from society and be forced to practice their habit alone or outdoors as the United States moves toward a smoke-free society by the year 2000.

From the time the Spanish explorers introduced tobacco smoking into Europe in the sixteenth century until the present, people have debated the effects of smoking. The issue of putting bans on smoking has shifted back and forth between antismoking and pro-smoking forces for over four centuries.

In recent decades, however, attitudes toward smoking have undergone their greatest change ever. The first U.S. Surgeon General's Report in 1964 warned smokers of the hazards of smoking, and a 1972 report warned nonsmokers for the first time that they risked adverse health effects from the smoke of other people's cigarettes and urged greater controls.

Today, almost everyone agrees on the harmful effects of smoking. But there are still many disagreements concerning the effects of smoking on nonsmokers and what, if anything, should be done to stop people from smoking.

———

Under a recent labor contract, the police department of Holden, Massachusetts, banned smoking both on and off the job by all newly hired full-time police officers. New officers are not allowed to smoke—not in the police station, not in a police car, not on the street, not even in the privacy of their homes.

The Holden police department acted for health reasons, noting that the last three officers to retire had done so on disability pensions because of high blood pressure or heart disease—ailments that are often linked to smoking. Two of the disabled officers—one in his early forties and the other in his early fifties—were smokers. Their disability pensions will cost the town $36,000 a year as long as the retired officers live!

The Holden ban on smoking raised some controversy. In the words of one police officer who favored the ban, "To ride in a police cruiser with a smoker for eight hours in the winter with the windows rolled up is uncomfortable." But according to a veteran of the force, who had been smoking for thirty years: "If a guy wants to smoke, that's his prerogative." Another, who agreed with him, added, "Beer drinking might be next, or eating eggs, because of the cholesterol. What the officers do off duty is none of the employer's business."

———

In 1986 the U.S. Army adopted a new policy prohibiting smoking in all army facilities, vehicles, and aircraft, except for specially established smoking areas. With the ban, the army put an end to the myth that soldiering and smoking go together. The army directive states, "Smoking tobacco harms readiness by impairing physical fitness and by increasing illness and absenteeism." An army spokesman put it this way: "About 52 percent of the 780,000 people in the active army are smokers. We are trying to get these soldiers fit."

Opposed to the new policy are the tobacco industry and its supporters. "It is unjustifiable, unenforceable, and unfortunate in its second-class treatment of servicemen," said Scott Stapf, assistant to the president of the Tobacco Institute, a group representing cigarette manufacturers.

Representative Thomas J. Bliley, Jr., a Republican from the tobacco-producing state of Virginia, said: "The army is moving too fast. I haven't seen any scientific information to back it up, and restrictions on smoking will hurt their re-enlistment efforts."

Representative Charlie Rose, a Democrat from North Carolina, another state that grows a lot of tobacco, commented: "There seems to be a steamroller, a bandwagon that the army has jumped on."

———

Today, when Martha Spencer, a cigarette smoker for twenty-two years, wants to smoke at her factory job in Suffolk County, New York, she has to step outdoors. Smoking is not allowed in the plant where she works. Not long ago, a county law went into effect requiring companies with more than fifty employees to ban smoking in work areas, as well as in restrooms, conference rooms, hallways, and elevators.

"I understand why they've done it," Mrs. Spencer said of her company's policy. "But it's a pain in the neck, especially in the winter."

The company's president explained the reason behind the new rule: "I'm a firm believer in protecting people against themselves. Employees were given the option of staying with us or leaving because of the new policy. Nobody left," he added.

Elsewhere, others are taking issue with the law, questioning Suffolk County's jurisdiction. Officials of one school system are openly defying the ban. Some school board members and some members of the audience smoke at school board meetings. Since the school district is a state organization, the board members insist that they are exempt from county regulations.

———

The USG Acoustical Products Company of Chicago, a manufacturer of tile and insulating materials, in January 1987 announced a total ban on smoking for its 1,300 workers in nine plants. Not only would smokers not be hired any longer, but current smokers would have to quit or risk being fired. The firm would monitor the workers through lung tests.

The company is apparently very concerned about its worker compensation costs. The risk of lung cancer is high among employees exposed to mineral fibers contained in insulation. The rate of disease is even higher among those workers who also smoke. At present, there are 112 asbestos-related suits pending against the parent company, USG Inc.

John C. Fox, a Washington labor lawyer, was one of many who were opposed to this action. He said, "Instead of cleaning up the workplace, they are placing the onus on the worker." Someone presently employed by the company put it more bluntly, saying, "I think it stinks. I put in my time, do a good job. What else do they want?"

Reactions around the country were generally disapproving. It was one thing to ban smoking from the workplace, many people felt, but quite another to dictate what could be done in a worker's free time.

About a week after the initial announcements, USG modified its stance. It announced that it would not summarily dismiss workers who smoked but review the situation on a case-by-case basis. And the ban applied only, it said, to those who work directly with the insulating fibers. Finally, the company said that the lung tests would not be used to monitor smoking but to check for possible disease.

———

Despite opposition to smoking restriction laws in the workplace, more and more businesses are adopting policies spelling out when and where their employees can smoke. A 1986 survey of 662 employers coast-to-coast shows that 36 percent of them have established policies on employee smoking, 2 percent have said they plan to put restrictions on smoking into effect before long. An additional 21 percent said they had smoking policies under consideration.

The most common explanation for establishing such restrictions was that they were required by state and local ordinances. Certain states, including Alaska, Connecticut, Florida, Maine, Minnesota, Montana, Nebraska, New Hampshire, New Jersey, New York, and Utah—have laws regulating smoking in private workplaces and many cities and counties have local ordinances.

New York City was recently considering a smoking-restriction bill. The bill, purported to be "most stringent," would ban smoking in many "enclosed" public places, including stores, taxicabs, public-hearing rooms, restrooms, waiting lounges, and

*An executive lights up a cigarette
at work. In the future she may not
be allowed to smoke in her office.*

semiprivate hospital rooms. It would also require restaurants, enclosed sports arenas, convention halls, offices, and factories to set aside nonsmoking sections. Violators would be fined between $200 and $1,000.

Both sides of the debate tried to shape the final bill. A summary of the testimony in this particular case can give an overview of the various pro and con issues involved in smoking of all kinds.

The Pro-Ban Issues · Proponents of the smoking restriction bill focus on health risks. They argue that the "best medical and scientific thinking" reveals that smoking harms not only smokers but also those around them. Numerous studies show that the smoke going into the air from burning cigarettes contains the same dangerous chemicals as the smoke being inhaled into the smokers' lungs. So-called involuntary, or passive, smoking is a health hazard that has been associated with lung cancer, heart disease, bronchitis, pneumonia, and asthma.

According to research figures cited by proponents of the ban, one person in the New York metropolitan area dies each week from exposure to involuntary, or "second-hand," smoke. A nonsmoking woman married to a man who smokes a pack of cigarettes a day is twice as likely to get lung cancer as a woman married to a nonsmoker.

Nonsmokers claim that they are being deprived of their rights by being forced to breathe second-hand smoke. People may have a choice about some things they do and places they go, but they have no choice when it comes to their jobs.

"We cannot force people to breathe smoke," said Joseph A. Califano, Jr., the head of the mayor's review committee that conducted the hearings on the New

York City bill. "That's not fair. Smoking is slow-motion suicide."

Any costs that business would have to pay to comply with the New York City plan are considered trivial compared with the millions of dollars the measure would save in health costs.

In general, nonsmokers see smokers as a group of selfish people who ignore the warning against smoking and risk endangering themselves and others. It is not the nonsmokers' obligation to ask smokers to stop, they say. Nor can they depend on smokers voluntarily stopping when there are nonsmokers in the same room. In any dispute, the health concerns of the nonsmokers should come first, they say.

The Anti-Ban Issues · Opponents of the ban contend that most research or data on the health hazards of inhaling the smoke from others' cigarettes cannot be substantiated. They say that many of the studies that link nonsmokers' health problems with exposure to smoke fail to account for other possible causes, such as the victims' own preexisting histories of smoking, lung cancer, or heart trouble. Moreover, many problems—such as sore eyes, sore throats, and running noses—which are blamed on exposure to tobacco smoke may in fact really be caused by poor ventilation.

The tobacco industry lobbied hard against the New York City bill because it stands to lose financially if people are not permitted to smoke wherever and whenever they want. The industry's supporters include the city's restaurant association, the horse racing association, and labor unions. They say that compliance with the bill would cost business millions of dollars a year, that it cannot be enforced, and that it is overly restrictive.

Those who argued against the regulations also opposed it as government intervention into the lives of private citizens. They attacked the plan as unneeded interference with what they think is properly the business of companies and their customers and employees.

"We don't need more legislation," says Paul R. Screvane, president of a support group, the Committee for Common Courtesy, which is financed by the tobacco industry. "It's inane. Common courtesy can take care of minor disputes. Whenever people object to cigarettes, smokers can simply put them out."

Those against the ban also say that if there really were a demand for a smoking ban in offices, stores, and restaurants, the businesses would respond. To be successful, business must give customers what they want. Restaurants, for example, would provide nonsmoking sections in the same way they offer patrons sugar substitutes and decaffeinated coffee.

The New York State chapter of the National Association for the Advancement of Colored People argues that the bill is discriminatory against lower level workers. Executives could still smoke in their offices, where they would not be subject to the ban. But rank-and-file workers, particularly minority-group members, who share their work space, would be penalized, according to Hazel Dukes, president of the state's NAACP chapter.

Those against restrictions also say that it will be extremely costly to construct isolated smoking areas in all the public places subject to limited smoking. Further, it will be difficult and expensive, if not virtually impossible, they say, to enforce such regulations in the city's tens of thousands of businesses and recreation sites. Another consideration is the possibility of a strong, negative reaction, making the situation all the worse. And there will be more danger of fire as people try to smoke in secret.

The Debate Heats Up · The places where people can legally smoke are dwindling. Forty states and numerous localities now have ordinances against smoking on public transportation and in public places. And the 1987 regulations of the General Services Administration is expected to snuff out smoking in federal buildings across the country.

Passions are now running high about where and when smokers may light up. In a 1985 Gallup poll, 62 percent of tobacco users and 83 percent of abstainers thought smokers should refrain from smoking when nonsmokers are present.

An antismoking battle is now raging throughout the land. Before considering the issues in this heated campaign in greater depth, let us take a look at the rise of smoking and the arguments of the pro- and antismoking forces in the past. We'll see that it is not a new fight being fought today but one that has been going on for four hundred years!

TWO

SMOKING:
ITS BEGINNINGS

No one knows exactly when the first tobacco plant (scientific name, *Nicotiana tabacum*) appeared on earth, but some very old folk legends attempt to explain its origins. Among these tales is an ancient Huron Indian myth that places tobacco's beginnings very far back in history, to a time when the land was barren, nothing was able to grow, and many people were dying of hunger.

According to legend the Great Spirit sent a woman to earth to save the human species. The woman traveled about the land. Wherever she touched the soil with her right hand, potato plants sprang to life. Wherever she touched the soil with her left hand, giant stalks of corn shot up from the ground. Finally, with the land green and fertile with potato and corn plants, the messenger from the Great Spirit sat down to rest. When she got up, a new kind of plant grew in the spot where she had been sitting: the tobacco plant.

What is the true message of this legend? Some think it suggests that tobacco is equal in value to the basic foodstuffs of life. Others say it simply means that tobacco was an afterthought and that it sprang from humble origins and should be considered a lowly substance.

Is tobacco a great source of pleasure or is it an evil curse? A panacea or a poison? A sacred herb or a harmful weed?

Before getting to the current issues, let us trace the development of the smoking habit, from the late fifteenth to the late seventeenth centuries.

The Spread of Tobacco · Although the exact origin of tobacco is not known, smoking most likely began among the American Indians. Europeans first became aware of the custom when Christopher Columbus landed in the New World in October 1492. The first allusion to tobacco is found in his diary entry dated October 15, 1492: "In the middle of the gulf between these two islands . . . I found a man alone in a canoe who was going from the island of Santa Maria to Fernandina. He had food and water and some dry leaves, which must be a thing very much appreciated among them, because they had already brought us some of them as a present at San Salvador."

Although Columbus had no idea how the Indians used these "dry leaves," which were most surely tobacco, he did comment that they had a sweet scent and were wholesome. Later, some crew members observed the natives at religious tribal ceremonies smoking rolls of tobacco leaves with one end in their mouth and the other end set afire. According to accounts that the sailors gave, the Indians "drank" with pleasure the smoke of these crude cigars.

The early explorers also saw Indians of the Caribbean burning the tobacco leaves in hollow Y-shaped pipes, called *tabocas*, drawing the smoke through their nostrils. And Ponce de León in 1512 and Verrazano in 1523 are believed to have seen pipe smokers in what is now Florida.

An eighteenth-century
engraving showing an
American Indian smoking
tobacco through a pipe

Tobacco appeared to be a very important part of the mythology and folklore of the native Americans that Columbus encountered. They attached great religious and symbolic values to the substance. Smoking represented welcome, unity, worship of gods and spirits, and healing. The sharing of tobacco, by smoking a peace pipe, was an old Indian custom. Among some tribes the smoke was inhaled for the purpose of inducing a narcotic state during ceremonial rites. And the smoke was believed to have magical qualities. Some Indians, for example, blew smoke over their warriors to make them brave.

At first Columbus thought little of the tobacco and showed no interest. But he did take some of the dried leaves back to Spain with him—where the "holy herb" of the Indian became the "very stuff of the devil" according to the Spanish priests, who saw only evil in the practice. The first sailor to smoke some of the dried leaves from Columbus's first voyage was actually jailed by the Spanish Inquisition!

Nevertheless, the demand for tobacco slowly grew. During the early 1500s, ships returning from the New World to Europe often brought back loads of tobacco. Jean Nicot, the French ambassador to Portugal, popularized smoking in France, thinking that the leaf had some useful, medicinal properties. His name is memorialized as the root of *nicotine*, one of the main chemical ingredients of tobacco.

The sailors on the oceangoing ships and more and more people in Europe began to enjoy smoking. It gave them a pleasant, lightheaded feeling. These first smokers used tobacco from the West Indies and the Orinoco Valley of South America. All the present kinds of tobacco are believed to have come from these two varieties.

John Rolfe planted the South American seed in the rich soil of Virginia, thus beginning the highly profitable trade in the North American colonies. In time, fields of tobacco were planted all along the coasts of Europe, Africa, and America.

By 1575 the tobacco trade was firmly established, and the demand for tobacco could no longer be met by occasional shipments. Tobacco began to be sent abroad in a steady flow from the growing number of farms and plantations in the American colonies, as well as in Cuba, Trinidad, and Venezuela.

Devil's Weed or God's Remedy? · Right from the start, the Spanish clergy regarded tobacco with suspicion. Wanting to separate themselves from the pagan Indians, the Spanish priests called smoking abominable, a pact made with the devil. One Spanish priest, Nicolas Monardes, wrote in 1571: "The Devil is a receiver and . . . showed them the value of this plant so that they might see imaginary things and fantasies which it reveals to them, and thus he deceives them." Another warned that smoking was "the Devil's revenge for his Indian children upon the white man."

Doctors, too, were concerned about the spread of tobacco. Many arguments took place within the medical profession about the effects of smoking on the brain. Some doctors claimed that tobacco smoke filled the mind and dulled the senses. Others held the opposite view. They said that smoking clarified thought and kept one alert and sharp. Dr. Evard of London wrote, "Tobacco causes vomit and is an enemy of the stomach."

A man named André Thevet, who first brought tobacco to France around 1555 and later smoked cigars in Brazil, wrote of his experience: "The first use thereof is not without danger, before one is accustomed thereto, for this smoke causeth sweats and weakness, even to fall into a swoon."

While some were condemning tobacco as the devil's weed, many more were calling it "God's remedy" because of its supposed medicinal qualities. Father Monardes, who had associated tobacco with the devil, also described its healing qualities. Deeply inhaling the smoke, he said, could cure a bad cough. Henry Buttes listed the other curative effects of tobacco: "The fume taken in a pipe is good against rheums [discharge from the eyes and nose], catarrhs [inflammation of the mucous membrane], hoarseness, ache in the head, stomach, lungs, breast. . . ."

Despite the raging dispute over the health effects of tobacco, growing numbers of Europeans were acquiring the smoking habit. Old and young, men and women, even children enjoyed "the pleasant habit of smoking," as Count Corti wrote in his book, *A History of Smoking.* A certain number of people even took up the habit because of their belief in tobacco's healthful qualities.

By the second half of the sixteenth century, smoking was all the rage in Europe. People in Spain, France, and particularly England developed a taste for tobacco. Near the end of the century, tobacco had spread to Holland, central and eastern Europe, and Russia. Merchants introduced tobacco, but travelers, colonists, soldiers, and seamen helped its spread.

Sir Walter Raleigh (1552–1618), a favorite both of the court of Queen Elizabeth I and of the English masses, helped make pipe smoking fashionable. Some tell that Raleigh even convinced the queen to smoke a pipeful of tobacco, but she became nauseous and did not continue the practice. Still, she insisted that all of the ladies at court smoke a pipe at least once.

By the time of the Great Plague in 1665, the belief that tobacco could halt the spread of disease had grown very strong. Doctors prescribed it for a variety of ills. A doctor in London summarized the medicinal uses for tobacco leaves: "To cure headache, a green tobacco leaf on the head; for redness of the face, apply the juice or the ointment of the tobacco leaf; for a toothache, tie a tobacco leaf over the aching region; for a cough, boil the leaves and shake the syrup on the stomach; for stomach pain . . . apply hot tobacco leaves over the region of the belly and re-heat when they get cold." He went on to prescribe tobacco preparations for cancer, burns, wounds, worms, warts, corns, and bites by a mad dog!

Students at Eton and other schools in England had to smoke a pipe of tobacco every morning to protect their lungs against disease. Most of the negative beliefs about smoking seemed quite forgotten by this time. Its appeal was two-pronged: it was both pleasurable and healthful. Molière, the French playwright, wrote, "Let Aristotle and all your philosophers say what they like, there is nothing to be compared to tobacco."

Among the small minority who raised their voices against the growing use of tobacco were some who made fun of smoking. One writer, in a take-off on the supposed virtues of tobacco, wrote: "O sovereign tobacco! that art a medicine for every malady. It is wonderful in operation, and they say it will make a lean man fat, and a fat man lean. But I know it hath made many wise men to become fools."

As seventeenth-century chemists began analyzing the tobacco plant, they came to understand the power of its active ingredient, nicotine. Experiments on animals were showing that tobacco was a dangerous substance. The medical profession stopped prescribing tobacco and began pointing out its harmful qualities. Someone at the time even joked that a smoker's tombstone should read:

Here lies he who would have lived longer if
He had not choked himself with a tobacco whiff.

By the end of the seventeenth century, tobacco was
no longer considered a healthful medical drug. But it
was still widely smoked for pleasure and recreation.

THREE

EARLY OPPOSITION
TO SMOKING

During the seventeenth century, the pipe was being smoked throughout England. The better shops had a special section set aside for smokers. Here patrons could smoke a rented pipe that came with a bowlful of tobacco. People who could afford them bought manufactured pipes of silver or clay with silver trimmings. Others made their own out of clay (like the Indian pipes, except for the tiny bowl), or supplied themselves with a homemade walnut bowl with a straw stem. By whatever means, all who could get tobacco were consuming it by the pipeful.

When Queen Elizabeth I died in 1603, James I became king of England. James was considered impractical and unwise. France's King Henry IV is said to have called him "the wisest fool in Christendom." But James had some strongly held beliefs, including an overwhelming hatred of smoking in general and of Sir Walter Raleigh, its most popular supporter, in particular.

Smoking in England Under James I and Charles I · A year after he became king, James I wrote a highly indignant antismoking essay entitled "A Counterblaste to Tobacco." He pointed out that the "precious stink" had become an outrageous extravagance; that autopsies of smokers revealed their "inward parts . . . infected with an oily kind of soot." He ended by bitterly describing smoking with these words: "A custom loathsome to the eye, hateful to the nose, harmful to the brain, dangerous to the lungs, and in the black stinking fume thereof, nearest resembling the horrible Stygian smoke of the pit that is bottomless."

As a way of curbing the smoking habit, James I limited the amount of tobacco that could be imported from Virginia. The main result of the decreased supply was an increase in the demand for tobacco and a rise in the price. Pound for pound, tobacco actually cost more than silver!

In 1604 King James raised the duty tax on tobacco by 4,000 percent, expecting that the new tax would further reduce tobacco imports. The effect was again quite the opposite. The excessive tax spurred a rise in smuggling, led farmers in England to grow their own, and seriously reduced the amount of money in the treasury. Far from stemming the tide of tobacco use, "persons of mean and base condition" as well as "the better sort" smoked more than ever.

Reluctantly, King James accepted the failure of his policies. Realizing that people would pay anything to smoke, he adopted an "If you can't beat 'em, join 'em" approach. In England—and later in Italy, France, Russia, and Prussia—the governments took over the importation and sale of tobacco. They set up tax structures that ensured them a handsome income from tobacco. At the same time the taxes on tobacco eased their consciences for selling a product that already was being blamed for causing much sickness and disease, including insanity and sterility and birth defects in infants born to parents who smoked.

*In the 1600s, during the reign
of King James I of England,
many Englishmen, including
family men, practiced smoking.*

James I, the most rabid foe of tobacco, thus became the first one to derive a large income from taxes on it. But his hostility to Raleigh remained strong. In 1618 he had Raleigh beheaded. It is said, though, that Raleign smoked a pipeful of tobacco just before kneeling at the executioner's block.

To protect the king's tax income on imported tobacco, James I issued a royal proclamation in 1624 forbidding the cultivation of tobacco by growers in England. Foreseeing Parliament's objections, the king asked the College of Physicians for their opinion. They told him just what he wanted to hear: English tobacco was "very hurtful and unwholesome." It lacked the perfection of the leaf brought from the more southern parts of the world. Although many members of Parliament protested, there was little they could do. But, despite James's best efforts, English farmers continued to grow tobacco.

Charles I, who became king on the death of James I, disliked smoking as much as his father. Yet he continued the same policies on the import and retail trade of tobacco. Moreover, as another source of revenue, Charles required that tobacco shops be licensed.

The growth of tobacco monopolies under James I and Charles I aroused envy in other countries and vastly increased the price of tobacco. But the public in general refused to abide by the tobacco laws. Normally honest, law-abiding citizens, including members of the clergy and military, saw nothing wrong with smuggling in bushels of tobacco leaf for their own use and to sell.

Tobacco in America · Meanwhile, in Virginia, many colonists criticized the expanding tobacco production. They felt it tempted farmers to neglect sorely needed food crops. The Virginia Company, which had been chartered by King James to colonize the area, was unable to convince the colonists to give up growing only tobacco. As a result, many settlers suffered from a lack of food during the winter of 1610, and the period became known as the "starving time."

John Rolfe, one of Virginia's early colonists, began raising the first commercial tobacco crop in 1612. Soon after he developed an excellent method of curing (preserving) tobacco. Rolfe also set up a successful export tobacco trade, which gave the people of Virginia a means of supporting themselves.

Even as late as 1622, some directors of the Virginia Company regarded smoking as a passing fad and an end to its popularity would cause economic problems later on. They discouraged each new governor of Virginia from furthering the development of tobacco plantations. In various ways, they tried to curtail tobacco production.

By the end of the seventeenth century, though, the tobacco plantation system was firmly in place. The average plantation was large, up to 30,000 acres. It required huge amounts of labor and capital. In 1671 there were 2,000 slaves and about 6,000 indentured white servants working on tobacco plantations. Over the next decade, though, indentured white labor became scarce. By the end of the century, almost all of the field hands were slaves.

In New England, the settlers of Connecticut and the Massachusetts Bay Colony, who were much impressed by the success of the Virginia planters, also tried to grow tobacco. But tobacco planting and smoking in New England were soon suppressed. The sale of the substance by servants, for example, was absolutely forbidden. Servants were only permitted to use tobacco "upon urgent occasion for the benefit of health."

To help curb the "immoral habit," Massachusetts passed a regulation in 1632 ordering that no one smoke in public. Connecticut, sometime afterward, allowed no one under the age of twenty to smoke, required a doctor's prescription for beginners, and permitted smoking only in private homes.

Some suggest that the profitable tobacco farming and trade in the southern colonies made smoking readily acceptable in that area. But the North, which was gaining little economic benefit from tobacco, was much more sympathetic to the antismoking forces and therefore passed laws to restrict its use.

The Spanish Colonies · Unlike the settlers of Virginia, the Spanish colonists in Central and South America were able to grow as much tobacco as they wished. Spurred on by the increasing demand for tobacco, the tobacco planters in the Spanish colonies kept very busy. Inspired by the quick profits they were making, planters focused all their energies on growing tobacco. The result was overproduction and overstocked inventories in Spain.

In 1606 King Philip III of Spain issued a decree that restricted the cultivation of tobacco in Cuba, Santo Domingo, Venezuela, Puerto Rico, and elsewhere. Colonists had a choice—either grow other crops or work in the mines.

Eight years later, the restriction, which had not been very effective, was eased, and tobacco planting was again allowed. Now, though, all the tobacco was to be shipped in Spanish vessels to Seville, Spain. The sale of tobacco to foreigners was considered a crime punishable by death.

As with other such strong-arm tactics, the effect was to increase illicit trading and smuggling of tobacco. It also made Seville the world center for the manufacture of cigars and other tobacco products. And King Philip III soon joined the ranks of kings and customs officials who benefited from the tremendous tax income generated by the tobacco traffic.

Throughout the seventeenth century, the amount of tobacco grown continued to increase, as did the number of smokers. It was with good reason that the period was dubbed the Great Age of the Pipe.

Official Opposition to Smoking · As the consumption of tobacco rose in the seventeenth century, the anti-smoking forces also increased their power. Under their urging, in some parts of Germany and the Netherlands, as well as in Denmark, Sweden, Switzerland, Austria, and Hungary, legislation was passed that prohibited smoking, prevented domestic cultivation of tobacco, and restrained tobacco imports.

When death rates rose in Sicily, the excessive use of tobacco was blamed. The pipe was declared illegal. But when this tactic did not work, the Sicilian Council announced that all available tobacco had been poisoned by the Turks. Even this did not help. Apparently, Sicilians preferred risking death from smoking infected tobacco to giving up the habit.

The use of tobacco in the Near East and the Orient also became fairly widespread. The sailors who accompanied Captain Cook brought the pipe to Pacific Islanders, to whom smoking was unknown. Jesuit missionaries and Portuguese traders introduced the habit to China, Japan, and India.

The governments, though, opposed smoking. The emperor of China decreed that importers of the foreign weed be beheaded. In Persia, smokers and tobacco merchants were punished and tortured. A Mogul emperor of Hindustan wrote, "As the smoking of tobacco has taken very bad effect upon the health

*French ladies of the seventeenth
century smoking pipes*

and mind of many persons, I order that no one should practice the habit." He declared that anyone caught smoking would have his lips slit.

The Russian czar in 1634 also prohibited the use of tobacco. First offenders, whether smokers or sellers, were to have their noses slit. Persistent violators were to be put to death.

Reformers in Switzerland got several town councils to take steps against what they called the "epidemic of smoking." The Berne town council added a prohibition against the recreational use of tobacco to a list of police regulations. Smoking had the same penalties as adultery—imprisonment, the pillory, and a fine. A special Chambres de Tabac was established in 1675 to deal with offenders.

The Church · The earliest church attempt to ban smoking is thought to have been a law passed in Mexico in 1575. It prohibited smoking in any place of worship throughout the Spanish colonies. In part, this was directed against converted Indians. But later orders included missionary priests, who were forbidden from using tobacco before celebrating the Mass. Anyone who smoked prior to Communion was threatened with eternal damnation.

Pope Urban VIII, at the request of the dean of Seville, issued a stringent papal bull against smoking. Apparently so many members of the congregation and clergy smoked during the Mass that the church in Seville was filthy with tobacco juice spittings. The bull forbade the practice under pain of excommunication.

There is no evidence, however, that the pope opposed the use of tobacco. Generally speaking, the church seemed tolerant of smoking, except within the bounds and property of the church. A later order specifically banned smoking at St. Peter's in Rome.

Despite the best efforts of emperors and kings, town councils and popes, the smoking habit continued to thrive. Before the beginning of the eighteenth century, most of the antismoking bans were recognized as ineffective and were withdrawn. The strong needs of smokers, combined with the even greater desire for profits of the tobacco growers and merchants, created an apparently irresistible force to boost consumption.

FOUR

SNUFF, CIGARS, AND CHEWING TOBACCO

Tobacco use grew by leaps and bounds in the eighteenth century. Virginia and Maryland remained the main sources of supply; by the late 1700s the two states were annually exporting hundreds of millions of pounds of tobacco all over the world.

Newcomers to America were also producing tobacco in the territory that was to become Kentucky and Tennessee, and the French were developing plantations in Louisiana. Elsewhere, large tobacco plantations were being set up in South America, Asia, the Near East, and parts of Africa.

In those days, before the invention of cigarettes, almost all the tobacco that was grown was smoked in pipes. As time went on, though, new markets for tobacco began to develop. First there was a huge demand for snuff, a powdered tobacco that was sniffed into the nose. Then came a period when cigar smoking was very common. And finally, the tobacco habit changed again, this time to favor chewing tobacco.

As before, the antitobacconists raised their voices. They passed laws, wrote essays, and preached against tobacco from the pulpit. But this time they had little success. The reason was that tobacco had become socially acceptable. Even the richest and most "well-bred" people were using tobacco in one form or another. And in public, too!

Snuff · Tobacco snuffing, the first big smoking fad of the 1700s, became popular for several reasons. It was simpler than pipe smoking, its effects were more immediate, and the much-wanted sneeze always occurred within seconds, followed by a wonderful sense of well-being.

Nicot is believed to have sent snuff to France's queen mother around the middle of the sixteenth century. The Cardinal of Lorraine, a friend of Nicot's, encouraged the use of snuff at the French court around 1560.

Catherine de Medici and her sons used snuff for headaches, but by the time Louis XIII became king, in 1610, many in his court were snuffing for pleasure. The king tried to ignore the habit and his successor openly opposed it, but this did little to discourage the courtiers from taking a pinch now and then.

The snuff that was used in France was made by grating tobacco on a specially designed rasp. The powder was then sprinkled on the back of the hand and sniffed hard into one nostril and then the other.

At one time, snuffers rasped their own tobacco. Each one carried a box containing a twist of tobacco, a small rasp, a tiny folding knife for removing snuff from under the fingernails, and sometimes a small spoon for bringing the snuff to the nostrils without dirtying the fingers. As the habit caught on, snuff was sold already ground and carried in a smaller, more convenient box.

Snuff was used early on by the clergy. The practice spread from churchmen in Spain and Portugal to the priests of Italy. Pope Urban VII became an enthusiastic

A variety of ornate snuff boxes.
Many museums keep exhibits
of these beautiful boxes.

snuffer. Many clergymen placed snuff boxes on altars, where they could easily reach them for a pinch or two.

As the practice of snuffing grew, critics arose, especially within the church. During a series of hearings on the canonization of an Italian priest, the cardinals were told that the proposed candidate had been a snuffer. Those who argued against the priest said that snuffing was a sensual and pleasure-giving habit, not appropriate for a holy man. The priest, however, defended himself. He said that he used snuff only for pious reasons. First it kept him alert for prayers, and second it repelled the odor of sinners. Apparently he convinced the council, because he was eventually canonized.

In short order, snuffing filtered down from the aristocracy and clergy to the masses in Portugal, Spain, Italy, and France. Protestant refugees from France, called Huguenots, brought snuffing to Germany when they settled there. And Charles II and his large court brought snuff to London from Paris after they returned home from exile in 1660.

Some say the returning Charles II and his courtiers used snuff instead of pipes to differentiate themselves from the class of merchants and landed gentry who had acquired money and land in their absence. They also may have considered smokeless tobacco daintier and more elegant than puffing on a pipe. In any case, the form of tobacco used in France became a class distinction. Aristocrats snuffed in luxurious rooms, dressed in special jackets and lavishly embroidered caps. Members of the middle and lower classes puffed their pipes on streets and in coffeehouses.

All the while, opponents were raising warning cries against the use of snuff. "Snivelers and snorters" were cautioned that the powder would destroy their sense of smell and fill their brains with soot. What is more, they said, snuffing tobacco would cause apoplexy, dyspepsia, or nausea, and would ruin the vocal cords. One critic associated snuff takers with the magpie who eats everything and anything and soils its own nest. A snuff box was described as a Pandora's box, a potential source of all sorts of ills.

Defenders insisted that snuff was beneficial and especially improved the complexion. Case histories were produced that "proved" that tobacco powder had cured bronchitis, consumption, apoplexy, and other disorders.

Medicinal snuffs were advertised as cure-alls and remedies, much as pipe tobacco had been promoted in the previous century. One testimonial by a formerly blind man said: "On taking one small pinch . . . my eyes opened. I am now ninety-six, can read the smallest type without glasses by moonlight, and drink barrels of the most potent beverages without a dream of a headache."

Numerous brands of snuff were on the market in the eighteenth century. Outstanding artists were hired to design the labels. The many hundreds of attractive snuff papers attached to the tobacco packages in the 1700s could be considered the beginning of large-scale tobacco advertising.

In those early days of our nation, snuff was considered an article of luxury. When Congress first considered a tax on tobacco, it debated whether to tax the "poor man's" pipe tobacco or the "rich man's" snuff. The law passed in 1794 placed a tax only on snuff. The tax was exorbitant, being 8 cents, or 60 percent, of the usual selling price.

Toward the end of the eighteenth century, for no known reason, the habit of snuffing began to die out. The French may have given snuff up because they were beginning to move toward democracy and wanted to disavow all associations with the aristocracy. Although the habit lingered on a while longer in

England and America, snuffing began to be considered a great waste of time. Those who persisted were said "to be in arrears of the times."

The Cigar · As snuff faded from importance, the even showier cigar came to the fore. Although Columbus and his men had found the people of the West Indies smoking small, tight rolls of cured tobacco leaves, the cigar remained a rarity outside of Spain and Portugal until the early nineteenth century.

Some evidence for the sudden development of cigar smoking in England can be found in that country's cigar imports, which leaped from 26 pounds (12 kg) in 1826 to 250,000 pounds (113,500 kg) in 1830. The next generation, as Jerome E. Brooks writes in *The Mighty Leaf*, was "suffused with cigar smoke." Moralists formed new antitobacco societies, and new attempts were made to curb what Brooks calls "the furious fuming."

The growing desire for cigars favored Cuba and the West Indies, which shipped considerable quantities of cigars to European markets. Because of the expense of imported Cuban cigars, many settled for so-called "Spanish cigars," which were made in Philadelphia. The wrapper was from the West Indies, and the filler more likely came from Kentucky. Some of the Spanish cigars were so cheap they were given free to bar customers!

In Germany, police regulations treated public smoking, especially of the cigar, as a fire hazard and an unsanitary nuisance. There were occasional clashes between the police and smokers, but in the end, the smokers prevailed.

In poetry and fiction, the cigar was associated with dashing, manly characteristics. There was thought to be something daring and presumptuous about the

Cigar smoking became very
popular among all kinds of people
during the eighteenth century.

cigar. Although it mostly appealed to men, women were encouraged to smoke smaller versions, called "queens." But whereas some daring women experimented with queens, most refused to smoke cigars at all. Like many enthusiastic cigar smokers of his time, author Mark Twain boasted of his habit. He once said that giving up cigars was the easiest of all things to do—he had "done it a hundred times."

Tobacco Chewing · Using tobacco for chewing is thought to have originated among the Indian tribes of South America. Some braves, it is said, chewed a plug of tobacco as they went into battle. At close range, they would try to blind their enemies by squirting tobacco juice into their eyes.

The supposed therapeutic value of chewing tobacco was widely debated in universities in the eighteenth century. Meanwhile, many less well-educated individuals used the substance as a dentifrice, a material for cleaning the teeth.

In 1797 a Methodist clergyman, Adam Clarke, issued a tract addressed to "all Tobacco-Consumers" but especially to religious people. He begged them, for the sake of their health and soul, to avoid the use of tobacco. Clarke also maintained that it had become unsafe to kneel when praying because chewers had made floors unsanitary for the knees of the devout. Clarke's writing must have done some good because in a second edition of his work he wrote: "One thing I find I have cause of rejoicing in. The Spitting Dishes [hand-spittoons] are vanishing from the whole circle of *my* acquaintance."

The tobacco-chewing habit reached a peak during the presidency of Andrew Jackson (1829–1837). The congressmen were notorious chewers; the habit was considered folksy and down-to-earth and thus linked them to the common people. So widespread was chewing that one foreign visitor even suggested that the eagle be replaced with the spittoon as America's national emblem!

Charles Dickens on his tour of the States had the misfortune of being struck by a stream of tobacco juice from a nearsighted chewer. To his readers Dickens wrote:

> *Washington may be called the headquarters of tobacco-tinctured saliva. In all the public places of America, this filthy custom is recognized. In the courts of law, the judge has his spittoon, the crier his, the witness his, and the prisoner his, while the jurymen and spectators are provided for. In the hospitals, the students of medicine . . . eject their tobacco juice into the boxes provided for that purpose. In public buildings, visitors are implored . . . to squirt the essence of their quids, or 'plugs' . . . in the national spittoons, and not about the bases of the marble columns.*

Before the close of the eighteenth century, the United States was greatly addicted to tobacco in all forms—the pipe, snuff, and chewing tobacco included. Philadelphia and New York had the largest tobacco factories. Exports of snuff and other manufactured tobacco products kept mounting. The quantities shipped rose from half a million pounds (230,000 kg) in 1800 to over 17 million pounds (7.7 million kg) in 1860.

The Antitobacco Movement in America · Mostly because of its economic importance, the American tobacco industry until the late 1700s was free of the kind of reformers who attacked European smokers and snuffers. The first attacks against tobacco in the States were made by the famed physician Benjamin

Rush (1745?–1813). In 1798 Rush wrote on the physical dangers of tobacco and insisted that smoking and chewing led to drunkenness. His articles, though, are believed not to have made much of an impression on the public.

From 1830 to 1860, however, a group including the showman P. T. Barnum and well-known educators, clergymen, and physicians opposed the use of tobacco. Horace Greeley characterized the cigar as "a fire at one end and a fool at the other." Actions against smoking ranged from mild lectures and advice to passionate denunciation.

The American reformers maintained that tobacco inspired lust and depravity. In the words of Orson S. Fowler, "tobacco-eating and deviltry are both one." But the opposition's cause was made more difficult by the fact that many people in the highest levels of society had the tobacco habit. As an example, the wives of presidents Andrew Jackson and Zachary Taylor were both ardent pipe smokers!

In urging people to give up tobacco, some physicians occasionally exaggerated the sufferings of smoking addicts. One physician described withdrawal in a patient this way:

Ghosts and goblins, spooks and apparitions, haunt his brain; and snakes and serpents of all shapes, sizes, colors, forms, and lengths dance attendance around the room, each in dumbshow chanting the praises of Tobacco. He finds it almost impossible to think of anything but Tobacco; while every perverted, enraged, and rabid instinct is crying out, "A quid [cigar]! a quid! my kingdom for a quid!"

In the early part of the nineteenth century, Charles Lamb, the English essayist and critic, composed his poetic "A Farewell to Tobacco." But even after making this pronouncement he continued to postpone giving up the habit. To surrender his pipe, he said, he must have a *"quid pro quo,"* that is, something to put in its stead. Since he didn't have anything better to do, he said, he continued to smoke.

The status of smoking in America was about to change around the middle of the century. Before long the American Civil War would vastly expand the consumption of tobacco in the United States. And there were soon to be revolutionary transformations in the tobacco habits of the nation as the first cigarettes appeared on the scene.

CHAPTER

FIVE

THE ERA OF CIGARETTES

By the mid-nineteenth century, just before the appearance of cigarettes, it had become clear that little progress was being made in stemming the tide of tobacco use. There were more smokers in Europe and America than ever before. Few believed the horrible case histories of how people's health was being ruined by smoking; few were frightened by the bans or punishments in various countries; and few paid attention to ministers who preached against tobacco in their Sunday sermons.

The cigarette, a roll of shredded tobacco wrapped in paper, appeared first abroad, then in the United States. It was not really a new invention. A number of Spanish explorers had seen something similar—a hollowed-out reed filled with tobacco—in Mexico. This kind of reed cigarette was brought from Mexico to the Pueblo Indians in the area that is now Arizona and New Mexico. Along the way, other kinds of wrappers were used, probably corn husks at first, then paper.

For a long time cigarettes seemed to be a passing fancy that would soon be over. But within fifty years, the conquest of smokers by cigarettes was nearly complete.

Soldiers and Sailors · British soldiers first started smoking cigarettes during the Crimean War (1853–1856), a war basically fought between Great Britain and Russia. Since clay pipes were easily broken in battle and cigars were too costly, the British soldiers began smoking crushed tobacco wrapped in paper. When the war was over the British soldiers brought home their paper cigarettes. Many English people were eager to imitate the habits of the war's heroes, and large numbers of new smokers were soon clamoring for cigarettes.

Although the French and Americans also began smoking cigarettes, most regarded the new way of using tobacco as a novelty that was best suited to dandies or snobs. The majority of smokers hung on to their pipes, cigars, snuff, or chewing tobacco.

The Civil War gave a fresh impetus to smoking in the United States. Many young men first learned about smoking when they entered the army, since tobacco was issued as part of the rations of both Union and Confederate troops. Then, when they returned home, they introduced the habit to the people they knew. Large numbers of Northern soldiers became familiar with tobacco while fighting in the Southern states.

This temporarily marked the end of most anti-tobacco sentiment in the United States. It was not considered very patriotic to attack a habit that was considered necessary to the well-being of fighting men. After the war was over, few were willing to speak out against smoking, although some reformers urged a total ban on it. They tried to educate young people about the evils of smoking. One poem intended to be memorized went like this:

> "I'll never use tobacco, no;
> It is a filthy weed:
> I'll never put it in my mouth,"
> Said little Robert Reed.

"It hurts the health;
 It makes bad breath;
 'Tis very bad indeed.
 I'll never, never use it, no!"
 Said little Robert Reed.

But these efforts to curb smoking met with little success. New machines were being invented to manufacture cigarettes quickly and cheaply, and the rise of advertising campaigns and marketing strategies was spreading the cigarette smoking habit to people of all ages, backgrounds, and economic levels.

Full-scale Production · The first high-speed, completely automatic machines to produce cigarettes were patented in 1876. By 1884, cigarette production by machine was in full swing.

The sharp increase in the production and sale of cigarettes frightened the cigar manufacturers. The four leading cigar producers launched an anticigarette campaign. They claimed that cigarettes were laced with opium and morphine, that the paper was bleached with arsenic and white lead, that the contents were tobacco scraps from the gutter, and that the cigarette paper came from Chinese leper colonies!

But it was not just the cigar manufacturers who were hostile to cigarettes. On January 29, 1884, the *New York Times* published an article that expressed a widely held opinion that the cigarette had a corrupting influence on users. "A grown man has no possible excuse for thus imitating the small boy. The decadence of Spain began when the Spaniards adopted cigarettes, and if this pernicious practice obtains among adult Americans the ruin of the Republic is close at hand."

Nevertheless, the sales of cigarettes continued to soar, and competition among American producers grew fierce. In 1890 the producers joined forces for the first time to promote their common concerns. This led the tobacco farmers to fight back. In 1904 they formed a "protective association" to look out for their interests. This group wrecked tobacco factories, destroyed crops, and whipped and murdered planters who would not join them. Many lawsuits against the association led to its decline, and around 1915 it was disbanded. The giant tobacco cartels established complete control over the growth, manufacture, and sale of tobacco in this country.

America Turns Anticigarette · By the end of the nineteenth century, the cigarette manufacturers were selling about 5 billion cigarettes a year. As the use of the cigarette rapidly grew, new antismoking campaigns began. The anticigarette groups were able to convince officials in twenty-six states to enact laws that made it a crime to sell cigarettes to minors. In practical terms, though, these laws did little to curb smoking among teenagers. The police were quite lax about enforcing the laws, and young people who wanted to smoke had little trouble getting cigarettes.

The lack of enforcement and the continued use of cigarettes led to the passage of even stricter laws. By the end of 1909, fifteen states had passed legislation that completely banned the sale of cigarettes. Two more states, Tennessee and West Virginia, placed such heavy taxes on cigarettes that the result was the same as a prohibition against their sale. New York City banned smoking on subways, trolley cars, and ferries.

The struggle between smokers and their opponents was also waged on the literary front. Many novelists and poets seemed clearly on the side of the tobacco users. Robert Louis Stevenson advised women readers never to marry a "teetotaller or a

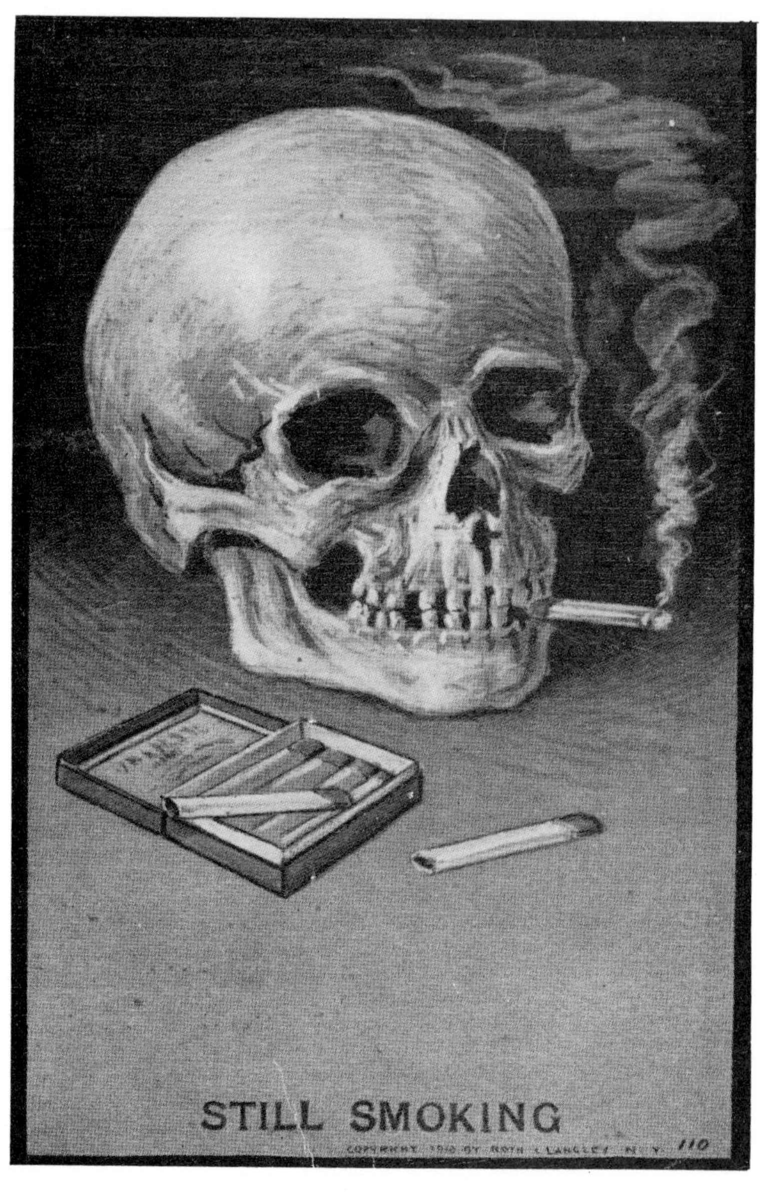

An early antismoking
propaganda picture showing
a skull with a cigarette

man who does not smoke." Smokers, he said, made the most contented husbands. James M. Barrie, the author of *Peter Pan*, produced a tribute to pipe smokers in his book, *My Lady Nicotine* (1890).

And there is this ditty by Graham Lee Hemminger from *Tobacco* (1915):

Tobacco is a dirty weed. I like it.
It satisfies no normal need. I like it.
It makes you thin, it makes you lean.
It takes the hair right off your bean.
It's the worst darn stuff I've ever seen. I like it.

One group opposed cigarettes but approved of cigar and pipe smoking. This group considered cigarette smoking to be bad manners and a sign of a poor upbringing. Men who smoked cigarettes instead of pipes or cigars were considered effeminate, and women who smoked cigarettes were thought to be vulgar.

Educators made up a large anticigarette group. Teachers lectured, wrote articles, and gave speeches that came down strongly against smoking. School boards issued official anticigarette position papers. They also invited speakers to address the students and organized anticigarette campaigns. It is said that they even encouraged children to snatch cigarettes, as well as pipes and cigars, from smokers' lips!

One particularly zealous worker against youngsters' smoking was Charles Hubbell, president of New York City's Board of Education in 1893. Believing that smoking was the cause of most behavior problems in young boys, he set up the Consolidated Anticigarette League in the city's schools. He got 25,000 boys to pledge that they would not smoke until they were twenty-one years old. The irony of Mr. Hubbell's position is that he himself was a smoker!

But educators were not the most powerful antismoking group. That position was held by the so-called reformers, of whom the most effective was Lucy Page Gaston.

Lucy Gaston was born in 1860 in Illinois. Her parents were very active in several reform movements—against slavery, alcohol, and smoking. While she was still a teenager, Gaston joined the Women's Christian Temperance Union, an organization that opposed the sale and drinking of alcoholic beverages, and became a hardworking member of her local chapter.

After earning a degree in education, Gaston taught school for several years. Often she would catch students sneaking out of school to grab a few puffs on a cigarette. She claimed that these were always her worst students. Based on her experience, Gaston said she could recognize a "cigarette face," the particular "look" of someone who smoked cigarettes. And she knew all the steps on the road to ruin that follow cigarette smoking: drinking, then sickness, followed by a life of crime to support the smoking and drinking habits, and finally a horrible death, leaving widows and children destitute.

After ten years of teaching, Gaston started writing for a newspaper in the town of Harvey, Illinois. Her first articles attacked the sale of alcohol. But soon she became an even more ardent antismoking advocate because she was convinced that cigarette smoke was more dangerous than alcohol.

Whereas some said that nicotine was the big danger in cigarettes, Gaston insisted it was a chemical called furfural, which she said was produced when tobacco is burned. The deadly furfural, she claimed, was fifty times more poisonous than alcohol. (Curiously enough, Gaston rarely included cigars, pipes, snuff, or chewing tobacco in her antismoking diatribes.)

In 1899 Gaston founded the Chicago Anti-cigarette League. The reform spirit was in the air, and large numbers of enthusiastic men and women joined the movement. Local chapters formed, first in the Midwest and then spreading out to both coasts. By 1901, the organization became known as the National Anti-cigarette League. In 1911, with the addition of a number of Canadian branches, it became the Anti-cigarette League of America.

The league found support for its position in the medical profession. Dr. L. Pierce Clark wrote that tobacco affected the brain, spinal cord, and nervous system. Others pointed out decreased mental ability, nicotine poisoning, elevated blood pressure, insomnia, and difficulties in breathing caused by irritation of the lungs and bronchial tubes. As early as 1912 a medical journal reported the following: "No physician doubts that smoking may be a factor in almost any disease from which his patient is suffering."

During those early years the league flourished. It set up clinics in cities across the United States and Canada, where people could come for a cigarette cure. A medicine patented by Dr. D. H. Hess, general secretary of the league, was used to kill the desire for cigarettes. The medicine was a weak solution of silver nitrate. In some cases, a physician swabbed the clients' throat with the solution. This made them ill if they smoked. Others were told to gargle with the solution after every meal for three days, soak in warm baths daily, and switch to a bland diet.

The league also launched antismoking campaigns that dealt with the moral objections to tobacco use. One, called No-to-bac, had as its motto "Don't tobacco-spit your life away." Another involved hiring a special private police force to apprehend and arrest anyone under the age of eighteen they caught smoking in public.

Concerning the breakdown of character and morality that resulted from cigarette smoking, perhaps Charles Hubbell, of the New York City Board of Education, put it best. He said in 1904 that smoking cigarettes "is more devastating to the health and morals of young men than any habit or vice that can be named." Further, he noted that the police and judges "have stated again and again that the majority of juvenile delinquents appearing before them are cigarette fiends, whose moral nature has been warped or destroyed through the instrumentality of this vice."

The arguments based on health effects and morality were those heard most often. But there was a third point, one that focused on the rights of nonsmokers. This position was the central thrust of the Non-Smokers' Protective League of America, a group organized by Dr. Charles Pease, a leading anticigarette reformer. In a letter to the *New York Times* on November 10, 1911, Dr. Pease stated the group's position: "The right of each person to breathe and enjoy fresh and pure air—air uncontaminated by unhealthful or disagreeable odors and fumes is a constitutional right, and cannot be taken away by legislatures or courts, much less by individuals pursuing their own thoughtless or selfish indulgence."

For a while the efforts of the anticigarette reform movement showed signs of being effective. Between 1897 and 1901, the number of cigarettes smoked dropped from just under 5 billion to below 3.5 billion. But some said it was the economy, not the reformers, that caused cigarette consumption to fall. The 1890s were hard times in the United States; many men switched from expensive cigars to cheaper cigarettes. Then, with the return of prosperity at the turn of the century, cigarette smokers returned to their favorite form of tobacco, the cigar.

The figures seem to bear this out. Cigar sales hovered between 4 and 5 billion all during the 1890s. For the first time, sales of cigars topped 5 billion in 1900, and the number soared to over 6 billion the following year.

Then again, it may have been American business, not the reformers, that reduced the ranks of cigarette smokers around 1900. According to this view, the antismoking campaign had made little progress until it received the backing of the country's business community. Factory and store owners achieved the desired result in a simple way—they refused to hire smokers. This led a number of states and cities to restrict smoking in various ways. As the *New York Times* wrote on August 8, 1907, "Business . . . is doing what all the . . . anti-cigarette specialists could not do."

Smokers Strike Back · While antismoking groups were at the height of their power, in the first decades of the century, various prosmoking advocates were working to halt what they saw as a threat to their right to smoke whenever and wherever they wanted.

As would be expected, the rich and powerful cigarette companies led the fight on behalf of the smokers. It is believed that the cigarette manufacturers paid lawyers to challenge the constitutionality of the anti-cigarette laws that were being passed on all levels of government. It is also said that the manufacturers lobbied the different legislative bodies, urging them to vote against any measures that restricted the freedom of smokers.

One of the few actions that is documented involved the United Cigar Stores Company in New York City. This chain of tobacco shops collected 72,000 signatures on petitions asking that smoking be permitted on subways and streetcars. The matter was discussed by the city's Public Service Commission on October 12, 1913, but the petition was denied.

Some of the strongest opposition to the bans on smoking came from people who were against smoking but felt it was wrong to pass laws controlling people's habits. Several newspapers and magazines came out against the anticigarette laws, calling them "foolish" and "fussy."

A number of physicians disputed the claims of the anticigarette reformers and educators. "What right does Lucy Gaston have to discuss the health effects of smoking?" they asked. "She has no medical degree or background to make such statements." In a 1913 magazine article, Dr. Leonard K. Hirshberg, a doctor at Johns Hopkins University Hospital, quoted "a physician of worldwide reputation" as saying, "I have yet to see, in either clinic or a pathological laboratory, any evidence to condemn tobacco in any form, not excepting cigarettes." Although Dr. Hirshberg agreed that boys and young men might be harmed by smoking, he felt that grown men would suffer no ill effects.

The greatest blow against the anticigarette forces proved to be World War I (1914–1918). As General John J. Pershing, who led the U.S. Army in Europe, said, "You ask me what we need to win this war. I answer tobacco as much as bullets."

Most of the young men entering the army or navy became heavy smokers. They were given a never-ending supply of cigarettes. Once again, smoking came to be identified with patriotism and love of country. In fact, when some reformers openly opposed sending cigarettes to the troops overseas, it was suggested that they be arrested and tried as traitors! The "cigarette fiends" of a few years earlier became men of "courage and dedication." In the face of widespread acceptance of cigarettes during World War I, the antismoking forces withdrew until the war ended in 1918.

The Pendulum Swings Back and Forth · One of the first issues in the smoking controversy to emerge after the war was: "Is it proper for women to smoke?" Many people of both sexes, including a good number of government officials, were opposed to women smoking. A law was introduced into Congress to make it a crime for women to smoke in Washington, D.C., but it was defeated. A woman in New York City was arrested for smoking a cigarette on the street. At trial the case was dismissed.

Around this time, the antismoking people scored some victories. Two states, Utah and Idaho, passed laws prohibiting the sale of cigarettes. There were also angry protests against the bad manners of cigarette smokers, women as well as men, in crowded rooms and restaurants. Many people disliked the way young people looked with cigarettes dangling from their lips and were concerned over the increased chance of fires caused by careless smokers.

Some church groups, including Methodists, Presbyterians, and Baptists, agitated against smoking during the 1920s. Their positions ranged from a Methodist tract saying that women who smoked were a "menace to the nation" to the Baptist hope to "wholly banish the use of cigarettes."

The medical profession held essentially the same position as it did before the war, but research raised a few new health concerns. Among them were the dangers of lip cancer from smoking and the bad effects on babies born to mothers who smoked.

Lucy Page Gaston, still the leading figure in the movement to stop cigarettes, had further expanded her organization in 1919 to become the Anti-cigarette League of the World. She fought the cigarette menace as she had done before the war. But times had changed, and her tactics did not work. She was sued and served with several summonses. Ultimately, the league asked her to resign.

These setbacks did not deter Gaston. In 1920 she launched a campaign to run for president of the United States. When she was unable to garner enough support she withdrew and again returned to her anticigarette efforts, which came to a halt with her death in 1924.

During the years following World War I, the tobacco interests became much better organized and presented their side of the controversy more effectively. The tobacco farmers and cigarette manufacturers set up special industrywide groups to counterattack the antismoking crusaders. The smokers themselves also came together to protect their rights. The biggest nationwide organization was the Smokers Against Tobacco Prohibition.

As before, many leading newspapers and magazines joined in opposing the anticigarette legislation. Using doctors' statements to back them up, they denied the health hazards of smoking. They also focused on the civil rights issue, saying that the anticigarette laws were improperly infringing on the smokers' constitutional liberties.

A new argument was based on the tobacco industry's contribution to the American economy. Growing the tobacco, selling, curing, and preparing the leaves; manufacturing the cigarettes and other tobacco products; and then shipping and retailing the cigarettes, cigars, pipe tobacco, snuff, and chewing tobacco pro-

Both men and women are being encouraged to smoke in this early cigarette advertisement, which glamorizes the smoking habit.

EGYPTIAN
DEITIES
"The Utmost in Cigarette
Plain End or Cork Tip

People of culture and
refinement invariably
PREFER Deities
to any other cigarette.
25¢
Anargyros
Makers of the Highest Grade Turkish
and Egyptian Cigarettes in the World

S. ANARGYROS
EGYPTIAN DEITIES
FORMERLY MADE BY
Anargyros
Egyptian DEITIES
TRADE MARK REGISTERED
No. 3 SUPERFINE
FACTORY AND DEPOT NEW YORK

vided many thousands of jobs. And, of course, the tobacco industry contributed millions of tax dollars to the government every year.

By 1927 the national attitude toward smoking had changed considerably. It became much more acceptable for women to be seen smoking in public. Most of the antismoking laws had been struck down. Idaho repealed its anticigarette law in the same session it was enacted. An antitobacco constitutional amendment that was introduced to the voters of Oregon in 1930 was rejected. The laws that remained did not affect the consumption of tobacco but chiefly prohibited the sale of tobacco to minors.

World War II · At no time did the antismoking movement seem more hopeless than during World War II (1939–1945). As in the Civil War and World War I, the soldiers took up the smoking habit with great enthusiasm. From the armed forces the acceptance of smoking spread throughout the nation. In fact, so great was the demand for cigarettes during the war that there was actually a tobacco shortage!

By the end of the war, smoking was rampant. Sales of tobacco were at an all-time high. Radios, magazines, newspapers, billboards—all carried colorful, catchy, and entertaining advertisements for cigarettes. Few questioned the idea of women smoking any longer. Rather, in movies and books, smoking a cigarette was considered very sexy and attractive. Tobacco reform seemed a lost cause. But not for long!

PART II
ISSUES

SIX

HEALTH EFFECTS OF SMOKING

Cigarette smoking is the greatest preventable cause of illness, disability and premature death in this country. Surgeon General

No other single factor kills so many Americans as cigarette smoking.
New York State Commissioner of Health

Cigarette smoking is one of the greatest threats to well-being in modern times.
California Director of Health

Cigarette smoking is the major known cause of cancer deaths. American Cancer Society

Cigarette smoking is a major factor in coronary heart disease. American Heart Association

Cigarette smoking is a serious health hazard.
American Medical Association

The health hazard of smoking is an accepted medical fact. American Public Health Association

Research in Smoking and Health · The first significant scientific connection between smoking and disease was made in the years just before World War II. Some surveys done in the late 1930s showed that many patients with lung cancer were also heavy tobacco users. This led the researchers to wonder if lung cancer was perhaps linked to smoking. As the evidence piled up it became clear that the rising incidence of lung cancer was related to the increase in smoking, especially of cigarettes.

Along with further confirmation of the smoking–cancer link, there was a growing suspicion that smoking had additional bad health effects. Studies released in 1934 and 1951, for instance, reported that cigarette smoking caused a drop in the temperature of smokers' fingers and toes from 5 to 15 degrees F (3 to 10 degrees C).

The explanation is that smoking causes small blood vessels, called arterioles, to narrow. This cuts down the flow of blood and leads to the drop in temperature of the extremities. In some cases, it results in the formation of a clump or clot of blood. The clot can stop the flow of blood and cause Buerger's disease, a condition that may require the amputation of toes or fingers. In some extreme cases it can even require the surgical removal of legs or arms.

Seven major studies done between 1951 and 1959 provide the main data on the death rates of male smokers. The population groups studied included British doctors, American and Canadian veterans, and some other groups. A major finding of these studies was that death rates from all causes are considerably higher for men who smoke than for men who do not smoke. In one project these rates ran about twice as high for male smokers aged forty-five to sixty-four as it did for nonsmokers of the same ages. In addition, the lung cancer death rate for cigarette smokers was ten times as great.

A much larger study (1960–1966) of more than one million American men and women over age thirty, who were alike in every way except for their smoking habits, found that twice as many smokers had died as nonsmokers—1,385 against 662. There were 110 lung cancer deaths among the cigarette smokers, contrasted with only 12 among nonsmokers. Six hundred fifty-four smokers died of coronary heart disease compared with 304 nonsmokers. Other striking differences were in the death rates from emphysema and cancers of the mouth, pharynx, larynx, esophagus, pancreas, and bladder.

On June 1, 1961, the heads of the leading health organizations in the United States sent a letter to President John F. Kennedy outlining some of the health dangers of cigarette smoking. Urging that "appropriate health measures" be taken, they requested that he appoint a commission to consider further action. A few days later, the surgeon general established a committee to review all data on smoking and health.

Around the beginning of 1964, the committee of eleven scientists issued a report called *Smoking and Health*. The report listed a number of conclusions: Cigarettes cause a wider variety of diseases than had ever been realized; excessive use of tobacco is a major health hazard in the United States; cigarette smoking is a major cause of lung cancer; smoking is a contributing cause of heart disease, chronic bronchitis, and emphysema; and death rates are higher for smokers than for nonsmokers. A month after the report came out, an association of health, educational, and governmental agencies took on the job of informing the public of the harmful effects of smoking.

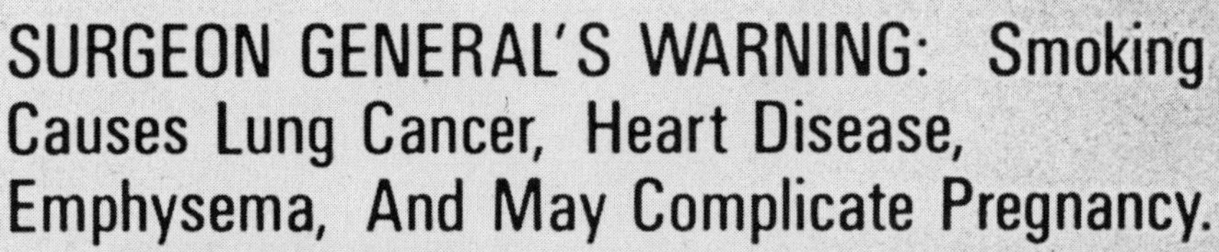

This is one of the warning labels that appear on cigarette packages today.

Harmful Substances in Tobacco Smoke · Few people realize that the temperature of a burning cigarette may be as high as 1,616 degrees F (880 degrees C). This tremendous heat releases a number of gases, including several that are poisonous and some that are known to cause cancer.

Carbon monoxide (CO) is a highly toxic, colorless, odorless gas. Researchers have found CO in concentrations as high as 40,000 parts per million in cigarette smoke. The maximum concentration allowed in indoor air under government regulations is only 50 parts per million.

The CO in the air is breathed into the lungs. Here it is picked up by the body's blood cells about ten times as fast as oxygen. As a result, the body is deprived of the oxygen it needs.

The first symptoms of CO poisoning experienced by cigarette smokers are the inability to perform strenuous activity and a shortness of breath. If the level of CO in the blood reaches around 30 percent, the smoker may become nauseous, dizzy, and suffer from headaches. At a level of 60 percent or higher damage to the brain and heart occurs, and death can follow in just a few minutes.

Most smokers do not suffer the deadly effects of CO poisoning because they take in huge quantities of fresh air along with the CO. But if they smoke cigarettes in small, airtight, smoke-filled rooms, the CO in the blood can indeed rise to a dangerous level.

The other major gas created in smoking cigarettes is hydrogen cyanide (CHN). This, too, is highly injurious. The government limit is ten parts per million. Cigarette smoke may contain nearly two hundred times that concentration. In small amounts CHN can irritate the throat, sting the eyes, and cause breathing difficulty. In larger amounts it causes giddiness and headaches. Maximum amounts can lead to convulsions, stoppage of breathing, and death.

Nitrogen dioxide (NO_2) is not a poisonous gas in most concentrations, but it is a powerful irritant. It chafes the lungs and the mucous membranes. In addition, it causes bad reactions in the skin and eyes. The government set a safety level of exposure to NO_2 of 5 parts per million. Cigarette smoke contains 250 parts per million.

In addition to forming gases, burning tobacco also releases many billions of tiny particles. All together these make up what is called cigarette or tobacco *tar.* According to the surgeon general, cigarette tar contains about three thousand separate chemicals, many of which are known to be poisonous. Also, the 1982 Surgeon General's Report has an incomplete list of twenty chemicals in tar that cause cancer in laboratory animals. Although no one has identified the specific substances that cause cancer in smokers, experimenters have shown that painting the skin of a laboratory animal with cigarette tar can produce cancer in the animal within one year.

The tar in cigarettes causes the sense of taste and smell to be dulled. Many smokers also find that their appetites are reduced and that the tar stains their teeth and the fingers used to hold the cigarettes. It is this same tar, in fact, that gives smokers bad breath and an unpleasant taste in their mouths.

Probably the best-known ingredient of cigarette tar is nicotine, a colorless, odorless, oily compound with a particularly sharp taste. It is an extremely powerful poison. Under the trade name of Black Leaf 40, it is sold as an insecticide. An injection of just a tiny drop, 70 milligrams (0.002 oz), of nicotine can kill a human being.

Cigarettes contain between 0.5 and 2 milligrams (0.00002 and 0.00007 oz) of nicotine. Inhaled in a concentrated dose, nicotine can cause faintness, dizziness, nausea, and headaches. Many people who smoke for the first time become victims of mild nicotine poisoning and show these symptoms. The greater the concentration, the more severe are the symptoms, which can range from vomiting and diarrhea to collapse and death.

A major effect of the nicotine in tobacco smoke is to stimulate the nervous system. This is the "kick" that so many smokers enjoy. But the good feelings don't last. They are soon followed by depression. It is the need smokers feel for another cigarette to get over the depression that makes smoking addictive.

The exposure to the various ingredients in tobacco smoke causes some general bodily reactions. Even though regular smokers enjoy a cigarette, pipe, or cigar after a meal, research has shown that smoking actually interferes with digestion. Incidences of stomach ulcers are five times higher among smokers, and ulcers of the duodenum (intestines) occur twice as often. This is in addition to stomach cancer, which occurs 40 percent more often in smokers than in non-smokers.

"Smoker's cough" and "smoker's throat" refer to the coughing, irritation, and hoarseness associated with habitual heavy smoking. According to an old story, a tobacco company found a ninety-year-old man in Alabama who had smoked a pack a day since he was thirteen years old. The company offered him $10,000 to come to New York to be interviewed on a 9 o'clock morning talk show. The man refused. When company officials asked why, he explained, "I don't stop coughing until noon!"

The problem has to do with the millions of tiny, rhythmically moving hairs, called cilia, that line the bronchial tubes. The cilia push foreign matter, such as dust or pollen, up and out of the lungs. Cigarette smoke, though, interferes with the movement of the cilia; in some cases, it destroys them completely. Thus, particles in the air and in cigarette smoke can accumulate in the bronchial tubes, where breathing or respiratory problems originate.

A recent study of 179 boys—smokers and non-smokers—in a New Jersey preparatory school shows how smoking affects the lungs. Regular smokers had nine times as many cases of colds, bronchitis, and sore throats as nonsmokers. Occasional smokers had about two-and-one-half times as many respiratory illnesses.

Lung Cancer · Cigarette smoking is the major cause of lung cancer. Fifty years ago, lung cancer was a rare disease. In 1982, the American Cancer Society estimated that 110,000 Americans will die of this disease every year. Among men it is the most common cause of death from cancer, and the "epidemic" of lung cancer among men has now spread to women.

Cancer is a disease, or rather a group of diseases, in which the cells of one particular organ or part of the body multiply and reproduce much faster than normal. The cancer cells spread out and invade the healthy tissue surrounding the spot where the malignancy first appeared. These cells continue to move through the body until they take over a vital organ and the victim dies.

Scientists are still not sure exactly what triggers a cell to start reproducing without limit, but they have found a number of factors in the environment that can promote cancer. Among them are contact with certain chemical substances, radiation, viruses, and air pollution. But these factors are of little importance compared to compounds in cigarette smoke known as *carcinogens.* A carcinogen is any cancer-causing element, whether it be liquid, solid, gas, or radiation. The

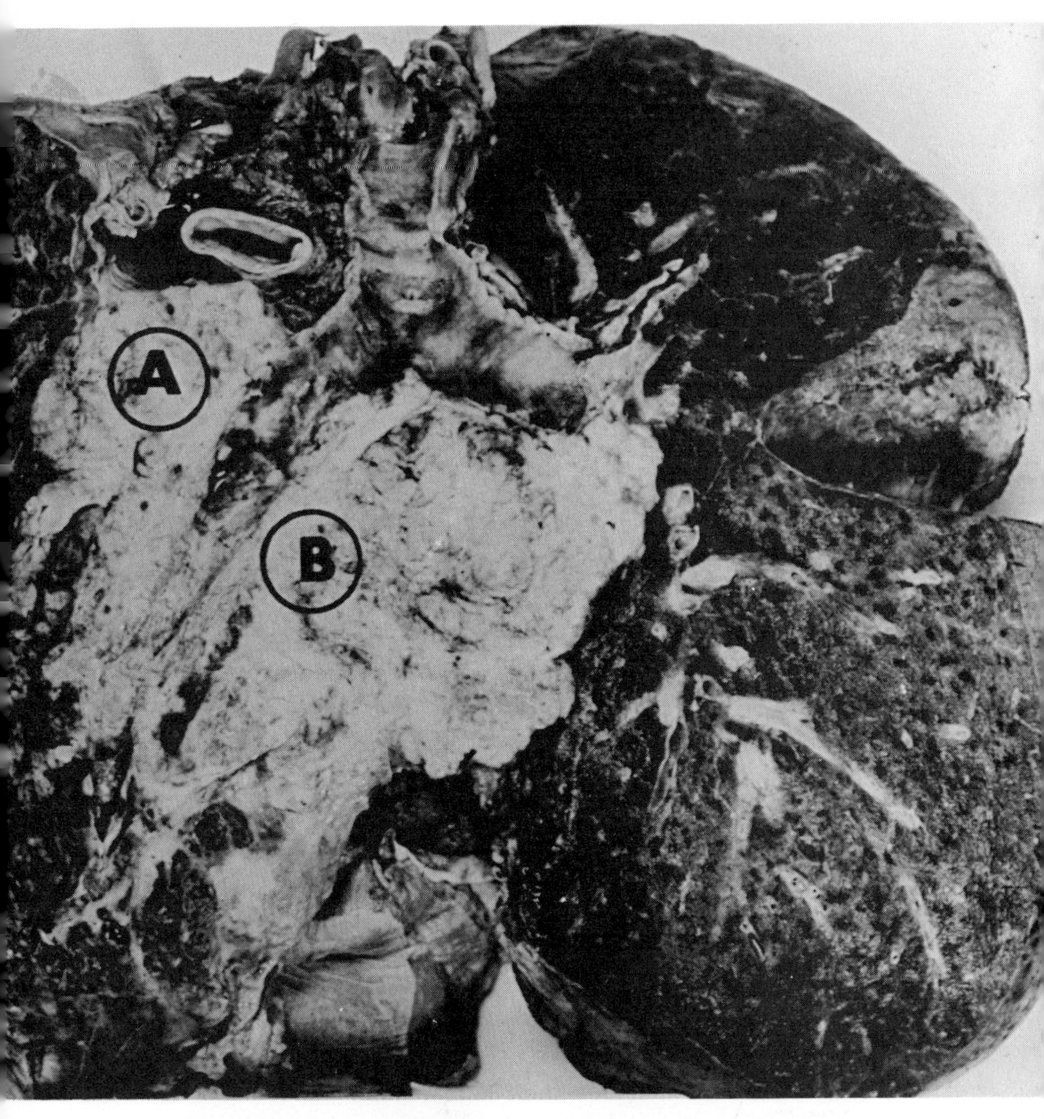

*Cross-section of the lung of a heavy smoker who died
of cancer of the bronchus. The cancer (A) has resulted
in a great narrowing of the lumen of the bronchus.
The tumor has extended beyond the wall of
the bronchus into the surrounding tissue (B).*

fact is that approximately 90 percent of all lung cancer cases occur in people who smoke cigarettes.

In a recent project, dogs who breathed cigarette smoke for up to twenty-nine months developed lung diseases similar to those found in humans. The lung damage was found to be progressively worse the longer the animals were exposed to the cigarette smoke.

Dr. Moses Barron of the University of Minnesota was one of the first researchers to become aware of the tremendous rise in the number of lung cancers. His study of autopsy reports at the university's hospital for the twenty years from 1899 to 1919 uncovered a total of four cases of lung cancer. Less than fifty years later, though, lung cancer was killing nearly two hundred persons a year in the same hospital.

Dr. E. Cuyler Hammond's five-year American Cancer Society study, 1969–1974, of one million men and women found that the death rate from lung cancer is higher among:

> smokers than nonsmokers
> heavier smokers than light smokers
> those who inhale more deeply
> those who started young
> those who continue to smoke compared to
>   those who stop.

Overall, according to the American Cancer Society, the chances of getting lung cancer are between nine to twenty times greater for regular cigarette smokers. A 1982 report estimates that 85 percent of lung cancer deaths could have been avoided if the victims had never smoked.

Smokers exposed to certain occupational hazards have an exceptionally high risk of developing lung cancer. One study showed that uranium miners have ten times the risk of lung cancer if they smoke compared to miners who do not smoke. Another study revealed that asbestos workers who smoke have a cancer risk ninety-two times higher than nonsmokers of their age in the general population.

Heart Disease and Circulatory Problems · Cigarette smoking is an important risk factor in the development of coronary heart disease, which is usually the result of an accumulation of fatty materials on the walls of the coronary arteries. By speeding up the damage to the diseased heart, cigarette smoking may bring on sudden death.

Autopsy studies of 893 men and women showed that those who smoked cigarettes only, or smoked and used alcohol, had more severe *atherosclerosis* (a thickening and hardening of the artery walls) than those who used neither cigarettes nor alcohol. The severity of the atherosclerosis increased in relation to the amount and the length of time the patient had smoked.

Heavy-smoking males between forty-five and fifty-four years of age have coronary heart disease death rates three times higher than those of nonsmokers. Women in the same age group who are heavy smokers have death rates from coronary heart disease twice those of nonsmoking women.

In addition to cigarette smoking, some other factors contribute to the development of coronary heart disease. The three major so-called "risk factors" are high blood pressure, a high cholesterol level, and excessive weight. Cigarette smoking can act without regard to these risk factors in causing coronary heart disease, but it can also work with them to make the risk of heart disease much higher. Thus, smokers who have one or more of these conditions have substantially higher rates of illness or sudden death from coronary heart disease. Those who are free of all three risk factors have lower rates.

Exactly how cigarette smoking affects the heart is not fully known. But nicotine and carbon monoxide both appear to be factors in producing coronary heart disease. Nicotine increases the demand of the heart for oxygen and other nutrients, whereas carbon monoxide decreases the ability of the blood to furnish the needed oxygen.

Cigarette smoking has other effects on the heart and circulatory system. For instance, both male and female smokers between the ages of forty-five and seventy-four have higher death rates from the circulatory disease commonly called stroke. Smoking is also a risk factor in the development of conditions such as Buerger's disease that affect the blood circulation in the arms and hands, feet and legs.

Respiratory Disease · Cigarette smoking is the most important cause of the group of respiratory ailments known as chronic obstructive lung disease (COLD) in the United States. Eighty to 90 percent of COLD is attributable to smoking.

Smoking promotes the development of chronic bronchitis and emphysema, two major types of COLD. A basic cause of both conditions is that the three thousand chemicals in cigarette smoke act as powerful irritants on the lungs and the bronchial tubes leading to the lungs. When the cilia are no longer able to perform their cleansing function, foreign matter can penetrate deep into the lungs, causing further irritation and increased mucus production, which can clog the air passages.

Bronchitis is a condition marked by an inflammation of the bronchial tubes. The cells lining the tubes are irritated, which leads to the buildup of large amounts of mucus. This further irritates the bronchial tubes, leading to more pain and discomfort. In an effort to get rid of the mucus, the person usually develops a chronic cough.

Emphysema, on the other hand, is characterized by great difficulty in breathing. The lungs lose their flexibility and elasticity so that they cannot suck in or force out sufficient quantities of air. In time, some of the lung tissue is actually destroyed. Emphysema usually grows worse with time.

Millions suffer daily with chronic bronchitis or emphysema. A good number of working men and women must stop working because of the disabling effects of these diseases. In addition, the death rates from the two conditions have been found to be nearly three times higher for light smokers than for non-smokers and twenty-two times higher for people who smoke one to two packs a day.

Heredity, air pollution, and exposure to pollutants and irritants in the workplace also contribute to respiratory illness. But when combined with cigarette smoking, these factors greatly increase the incidence of illness and number of deaths from the disease.

Coughing often precedes the more serious consequences of cigarette smoking. A persistent cough is usually the body's effort to get rid of something, such as excessive mucus. Coughing and mucus accumulations are both more frequent among smokers than among nonsmokers. Even college-aged youth show an increase in these symptoms if they smoke cigarettes.

Other Sicknesses · In addition to the major lung, heart, and respiratory diseases, cigarette smoking is also associated with the development of other illnesses. Smoking plays a major role in causing cancers of the larynx and the oral cavity, which includes the pharynx, mouth, and cheek. Cancer of the larynx is most often found in men in the fifty-five to seventy

age group. According to the surgeon general's conclusion in 1982, the risk of developing laryngeal cancer among heavy cigarette smokers is twenty to thirty times higher than that of nonsmokers.

An association has been established between the use of tobacco in its various forms and cancer of the esophagus. The 1982 report stated that alcohol consumption may interact with cigarette smoking. "The use of alcohol in combination with smoking acts . . . to greatly increase the risk for esophageal cancer mortality."

Research data have also revealed a link between cigarette smoking and urinary bladder cancer. Researchers estimate that 40 percent of male bladder cancers and 31 percent of female bladder cancers may be attributable to smoking cigarettes. One study indicates that smokers of more than twenty cigarettes a day have a death rate from this disease twice that of nonsmokers. An association also exists between cigarette smoking and cancer of the pancreas and kidney. Smokers have a higher risk of kidney cancer, ranging from about one-and-a-half to over five times the normal.

Cigarette smoking appears to be connected with increased illness and higher death rates from peptic ulcer, especially gastric ulcer. The number of cases of peptic ulcer have been found to be almost 100 percent higher for male smokers and more than 50 percent higher for female smokers than for those who have never smoked. Cigarette smoking also appears to interfere with the standard ulcer treatment and to slow the rate of ulcer healing. There is some evidence that smokers have more tooth loss, loss of bone in the mouth, slower healing after dental surgery, gum disease, and sores in the mouth.

Women who smoke during pregnancy are literally affecting two lives—their own and that of their unborn babies. Studies both in the United States and England show that among women who smoke when pregnant there is a greater number of low birthweight babies— that is, children who weigh less than the normal average at birth—than among women who do not smoke. In a study of 100,000 births, the smoking mothers' babies weighed on the average 6.1 ounces (173 grams) less than those of nonsmoking mothers.

There is also strong evidence that smoking mothers have a significantly higher number of still-births and have more babies who die in the first month of infancy, than women who do not smoke. The reason? Low birthweight babies have a greater risk of disease and death. According to the results of a recent research project, one out of every five unsuccessful pregnancies would have been successful if the mother-to-be had not been a regular smoker.

A follow-up study of smoking mothers' babies at the age of seven showed some marked effects. The children born to heavy smokers were shorter in height and scored lower in reading ability and social adjustment than the children of nonsmoking mothers.

In general, the death rates of pipe and cigar smokers are about the same as those of nonsmokers, provided that only a moderate amount of tobacco is consumed and the smoke is not inhaled. Those who smoke pipes or cigars frequently or inhale, however, have death rates higher than those of nonsmokers.

The risk of developing cancer of the mouth or esophagus is higher for pipe and cigar smokers than for those who do not smoke at all. It is about the same as for cigarette smokers. The chance of getting cancer of the larynx is three to seven times higher for these smokers.

A close connection has also been established between pipe smoking and cancer of the lip at the point where the pipe stem is held.

The Two Viewpoints · The sides are drawn in the argument over the health effects of smoking. Nearly everyone agrees that smoking is harmful. But whereas one group questions the cause-and-effect relationship between cigarettes and disease, the other firmly believes that smoking is closely linked to various diseases.

The Tobacco Institute and some others claim that the medical evidence is only statistical. Numerical facts or data themselves are not sufficient to lead to the conclusion that cigarette smoking causes lung cancer, heart disease, and the respiratory diseases, they say. In their opinion, the fact that lung cancer increased when cigarette smoking increased does not mean that cigarette smoking causes lung cancer.

Statistics, many experts insist, are the basis of most medical research studies. And all research, whether with animals or humans, uses statistical techniques to reach sound, scientific conclusions that are then accepted by other scientists. As the Royal College of Physicians points out in its 1971 report, *Smoking and Health Now,* ". . . it is possible to observe what is, in effect, an experiment in which millions of people who have been smoking cigarettes often develop lung cancer while millions of others who have abstained seldom do so."

The second objection that opponents make to the smoking/disease link is that the specific substance that causes cancer in smokers has not been identified. Therefore, the dissenters insist that it is unscientific to blame all the diseases on cigarette smoking. "The mechanisms by which lung cancer, heart disease, emphysema, and perinatal problems occur are unknown," the Tobacco Institute says. "No element the way it's found in tobacco smoke has ever been shown to be the cause of any disease in humans."

The scientific community replies that it is not necessary to know the exact cancer-causing agent in cigarettes to prevent deaths from smoking. Take the instance of curing scurvy in the nineteenth century. Doctors learned that the disease could be prevented by eating limes, even though they did not know that the underlying cause was a vitamin C deficiency.

Also, cigarette smoke is not a single chemical but thousands of different chemicals, many of them known to be harmful. Exposure to this range of chemicals, then, could well increase the risk of more than one disease. Exactly what parts of the smoke cause disease in humans is, in part, not known because of the obvious difficulties of doing research on people.

The prosmoking forces also argue that the smokers who get lung cancer may be born with a desire to smoke and a tendency toward the disease. According to this view, smoking is the symptom of a condition, not the cause.

Although some psychological and physiological differences are evident between smokers and non-smokers, there is no evidence of an inherited tendency toward lung cancer. When British doctors stopped smoking, their lung cancer death rate went down. This contradicts the premise of an inborn desire to smoke and an inborn tendency to lung cancer.

Still other theories claim that the rise in lung cancer is fictitious, caused by better diagnosis or from a fall in the death rate from tuberculosis. The facts, however, show that the rise is real, not just statistical. The rise in lung cancer has been greater in men than in women, and both sexes are diagnosed the same way. In addition, whereas the fall in the tuberculosis mortality rate has been greater in women, it has not increased in men.

SEVEN

HEALTH EFFECTS OF PASSIVE SMOKING

The combined epidemiological and chemical evidence suggests that the biological effects of passive exposure are real.
American Association for Cancer Research

The evidence currently available suggests that involuntary smoke exposure may increase the risk of lung cancer in nonsmokers. Prudence dictates that nonsmokers avoid exposure to second-hand tobacco smoke to the extent possible.
Surgeon General's Report, 1982

Involuntary smoking can cause lung cancer in nonsmokers. **Surgeon General's Report, 1986**

Indoor exposure to tobacco smoke has adverse effects. Involuntary exposure to tobacco smoke ought to be minimized or avoided where possible.
National Research Council

For many people, the main or sole exposure to numerous gaseous and particulate compounds results from passive exposure to tobacco smoke. Smoking is the major source of particles.
National Academy of Sciences

Physical Effects · Passive smoking, involuntary smoking, forced smoking, secondary smoking, second-hand smoking—all are terms that refer to nonsmokers who are forced to breathe in smoke from smokers in the same room. The 1972 and 1986 surgeon general's reports stressed the health effects of passive smoking, which can be as serious, or even more so, than the effects of direct smoking.

The amount of smoke taken in by involuntary smokers can be very considerable. Major research projects conducted in the United States, Japan, and Greece found that nonsmoking wives of smoking husbands each day inhaled cigarette smoke equivalent to smoking 5.8 cigarettes by themselves. Another researcher placed twenty-one smokers and twenty-eight nonsmokers in a room. The smokers lit a cigarette every fifteen minutes for an hour and a half. The figures showed that, if extended to eight hours, the nonsmokers would have had as much smoke as from smoking five cigarettes.

Dr. C. Simacek of Czechoslovakia did a study of 123,235 adults and found a significant increase in chronic bronchitis in the nonsmokers who were married to smokers. But curiously enough, the increase was greater in the nonsmoking husbands than in nonsmoking wives. The researcher believes that whereas husbands who smoke may avoid smoking near the wife when she is pregnant or caring for a young child, smoking wives are seldom under such restraints. The latest results from the Multiple Risk Factor Intervention Trial, a large study that is exploring ways to prevent heart disease, found that men who are married to cigarette-smoking wives were more likely to suffer from heart disease than the husbands of nonsmoking women.

Cigarettes produce two kinds of smoke. *Mainstream* smoke is the smoke that smokers pull through their cigarettes and into their lungs. *Sidestream* smoke is the smoke that curls up into the air from the burning cigarette. Typical smokers inhale ten two-second puffs of mainstream smoke from each cigarette. But the cigarette continues to burn for about ten minutes, releasing waves of sidestream smoke into the air during the nonpuffing times.

According to some scientists, sidestream smoke is even more dangerous than mainstream smoke. Two research reports bear this out. An article in the March 1978 *Journal of the Iowa Medical Society* states that sidestream smoke contains five times the carbon monoxide, three times the tar and nicotine, and up to *fifty* times the number of carcinogens found in mainstream smoke. A study reported by the National Institute of Environmental Health Sciences in February 1985 confirms that sidestream smoke contains up to fifty times more carcinogens.

Breathing cigarette smoke can aggravate the condition of people with allergies or with lung, heart, or respiratory problems. Sufferers with chronic bronchitis and emphysema, for instance, are made extremely uncomfortable by severe air pollution. Yet the levels of carbon monoxide and other pollutants in smoke-filled rooms may be as high or higher than those that occur during air pollution emergencies.

Even perfectly healthy people are affected by second-hand smoke. Their heart rate, blood pressure, and the level of carbon monoxide in the blood increase when they breathe in air full of tobacco smoke. Seated next to a smoker, a nonsmoker can be exposed to carbon monoxide levels more than twice as high as the maximum government standard. Also, even after nonsmokers leave a smoky room, it takes hours for the carbon monoxide to leave their bodies. Unlike oxygen, which is breathed in and then out again in minutes, carbon monoxide remains in the blood for long periods of time.

One or more smokers in a small room with little

ventilation can quickly bring the smoke concentration up to a high level. The demands on air conditioners in smoke-filled rooms have been known to jump up as much as 600 percent! Almost everyone present will complain of eye irritation and distress. To make it worse, tobacco smoke tends to cling to people and their clothing.

The *British Medical Journal* in 1982 reported that the nicotine level in the saliva and urine of non-smokers who worked near smokers was measurably higher than for other nonsmokers. Dr. J. L. Repace wrote that passive smokers suffer the same health effects as active smokers. His evidence, though, shows that passive smokers are at about the same risk as pipe and cigar smokers, which is lower than the risks for those who smoke cigarettes.

The April 1, 1981, issue of the *Journal of the Israel Medical Association* summarizes six groupings of health effects caused by breathing in second-hand tobacco smoke:

1. *Reduced efficiency of the lungs.* Passive smoking cuts the capacity of the lungs, making it more difficult to inhale deeply and to exhale with force.

2. *Increased risk of diseases of the air passages and bronchial tubes.* The small airways, in particular, are narrowed by passive smoking.

3. *Increased blood pressure and faster heartbeat.* The sidestream smoke has the same effects on the heart and blood system as mainstream smoke, though there is no evidence of permanent damage.

4. *Decreased motor abilities.* This is believed to be related to the increase of carbon monoxide (CO)

found in the blood of passive smokers. In one experiment, the percentage of CO in the blood of nonsmokers in a room with smokers rose from 1.6 percent to 2.2 percent. It is known that at CO percentages over 2, there is some interference with the body's motor functions.

5. *Irritation of the eyes, nose, and air passages.* The most frequent complaint of nonsmokers in the vicinity of smokers is the physical discomfort caused by exposure to the tobacco smoke in the air.

6. *Increased tearing, sneezing, runny nose, mouth and throat dryness, wheezing, tiredness, and dizziness.* These additional reactions to passive smoking are very common.

The groups of people who are at especially high risk from breathing another's tobacco smoke, according to the same source, include those with chronic heart or lung ailments; young children and infants; persons suffering with asthma, hay fever, or other allergies; and persons who wear contact lenses.

There is no complete agreement on whether passive smoking causes cancer. But in 1981, Dr. T. Hirayama reported the results of a mammoth study that involved 265,000 adults and lasted fourteen years. Here are some of his figures:

	Death rate per 100,000
Women not exposed	8.7
Passive smokers	15.5
Smokers	32.8

	Death Ratio
Women not exposed	1.0
Wives of moderate smokers	1.61
Wives of heavy smokers	2.08

The 1982 Surgeon General's Report says that there is an above-average rate of lung cancer among the non-smoking wives of smoking husbands. The 1986 Surgeon General's Report firmly establishes the idea that involuntary smoking can cause lung cancer.

Psychological Effects · Many studies have shown that passive smoking can cause psychological changes. In one survey on the effects of second-hand smoke on nonsmokers' attentiveness and learning ability, Drs. R. E. Shor and D. C. Williams interviewed 246 non-smoking students who attended colleges and universities where smoking was allowed in the classrooms. Nearly half (48 percent) said that the smoke pollution in the classrooms interfered with their intellectual performance and hurt their grades. About two-thirds (65 percent) claimed that the discomfort caused by the passive smoking grew worse at times of stress, such as before or during a test.

Some research results show that breathing in tobacco smoke can significantly increase a person's anxiety level. Those surveyed either reported being, or were seen to be, more worried, tense, and high-strung when in smoky rooms than when breathing clean air. There were also more instances of emotional upset during or immediately after passive smoking. And researchers noted more incidents of hostile behavior in nonsmoking subjects who were exposed to cigarette smoke.

Fetuses and Infants · When a pregnant woman smokes, the fetus or unborn child in her womb is really a passive smoker. Since the fetus gets all of its nourishment from its mother, some of the harmful gases and poisonous substances in the inhaled smoke actually pass from her blood through the placenta and into the fetal bloodstream. Recent evidence seems to show that the fetus is also affected if the mother is frequently exposed to tobacco smoke at home or at work.

One of the gases in smoke, carbon monoxide, deprives both the mother's and the fetus's red blood cells of oxygen. Nicotine adds to the damage by narrowing blood vessels, including those in the placenta itself. This decreases the amount of oxygen and food delivered to the unborn baby.

Most young female smokers (62 percent) surveyed said that they believe smoking can harm an unborn child. Although many either cut back during pregnancy (32 percent) or stopped for that period (35 percent), a high percentage returned to smoking after their babies were born. Apparently they did not realize, or were not convinced, that babies can also be harmed by the mother's or family's smoking.

Children of smoking parents are subject to an increased incidence of *all* types of disease. According to one major study, in their first year of life, babies of parents who smoke at home have a much higher incidence of lung disease, specifically bronchitis and pneumonia, than babies with nonsmoking parents. In comparison with older children and adults, babies have fewer defenses against substances they inhale, including pollutants and germs.

A recently published study in *The New England Journal of Medicine* showed reduced lung function in children whose mothers smoke cigarettes. There is also evidence that once lung disease begins in childhood, it can continue and even worsen over a lifetime.

Other adverse effects of passive smoking on

*In this situation where the pregnant
mother smokes, both the child and
the unborn baby are passive smokers.*

babies may be a higher percentage of deaths from sudden infant death (SID). SID, which is sometimes called crib death, is a frightening condition in which apparently healthy, normal infants suddenly stop breathing and die. Although scientists have not yet been able to pinpoint the cause, they have found that a much higher percentage of babies of mothers who smoked (70 percent) died from crib death than did babies of nonsmoking mothers.

The Two Viewpoints · In spite of the overwhelming evidence of the dangers of passive smoking, tobacco industry representatives attempt to discredit any links between exposure to second-hand smoke and disease. In their position paper entitled "Cigarette Smoke and the Nonsmoker," they state many of their chief points regarding the effects of involuntary smoking.

First, the industry criticizes the scientific studies and claims that the conclusions are not well documented. Many experiments, industry spokesmen say, were conducted under unrealistic conditions. Extremely high concentrations of tobacco smoke were released into small, sealed rooms, which would almost never occur in real life.

Further, they assert, there are so many pollutants and carcinogens in the environment that there is no justification for putting all the blame for the physical and mental harm on tobacco smoke. They also quote a 1975 study which showed that "a nonsmoker would have to spend a hundred hours straight in the smokiest bar to 'absorb' the [nicotine] equivalent of a single filtertip cigarette." No mention is made of the fact that nicotine tends to settle out of the air fairly quickly and therefore is not a good indicator of total exposure.

In some instances the industry bases its argument on selective quotations taken from papers written by distinguished members of the medical community. One such instance involved Dr. Claude Lenfant of the National Heart, Lung and Blood Institute. In its position paper the tobacco group quoted Dr. Lenfant as saying, "The evidence that passive smoking in a general atmosphere has health effects remains sparse, incomplete, and sometimes unconvincing." But reading the entire article from which this excerpt was taken gives a different impression. Referring to a new study, Dr. Lenfant went on to say, "Now, for the first time, we have a quantitative measurement of physical change—a fact that may tip the scales in favor of the nonsmokers."

The industry also minimizes the effect of cigarette smoke as a source of carbon monoxide in the environment. CO is often associated with heart disease. Yet members of certain occupations, they say, who are exposed to high levels of CO on a regular basis do not have excess rates of heart ailments.

What the industry fails to note, however, is that smokers in those occupations have more heart disease than do those who do not smoke. Thus, whether CO is the actual culprit is not the point. Cigarette smoke is the issue, and, as shown in the 1983 Surgeon General's Report, cigarette smoke can indeed cause heart ailments.

Most everyone, industry representatives and others, agree that cigarette smoking does cause disease. And more and more studies are now showing that passive smoking, or second-hand smoke, is also extremely dangerous. On the basis of this evidence, nonsmokers, health officials, and the nation's lawmakers are asking for laws that will restrict smoking in public places and in the workplace. Until it is proven safe, they say, everything possible should be done to avoid forcing nonsmokers to breathe in second-hand tobacco smoke.

But the prosmoking groups insist that such restrictions will curtail the freedoms of individual smokers and therefore of the population at large. They insist that until there is clear, definitive proof that passive smoking causes specific diseases, there should be no restrictions on smoking. Their motto is, "As much government as necessary, as much freedom as possible."

EIGHT

THE SOCIAL
ASPECTS

Most people are aware that smoking is hazardous. By the time boys and girls reach junior high school, one survey found, almost all of them believe cigarettes can harm their health. More than half of the young people questioned believe that one's health can suffer with only one year of smoking. Eighty-four percent of teenage smokers said smoking is habit-forming and a tough habit to break; 77 percent thought it is better not to start smoking than to have to quit.

But it is clear that fear of the effects of smoking are not enough to discourage millions of people from smoking. Many still do not seem to appreciate how dangerous it really is. About 30 percent of all adults in the United States continue to smoke cigarettes, according to the October 1986 figures of the American Cancer Society.

The federal Office on Smoking and Health estimates that about one in five teenagers smokes. Since 1979 more girls than boys, ages twelve to eighteen, smoke cigarettes. Those who are trying to prevent smoking are concerned, because the younger a person starts smoking, the more likely he or she is to smoke regularly and become a heavy smoker.

Why, then, do teenagers start smoking? Who can help get the antismoking message across? What can be done to stop smoking?

Family and Peer Influence · Many children between the ages of four and ten, researchers say, take the dangers of smoking quite literally. They worry when parents or siblings smoke because they know it "can cause cancer or a heart attack." Yet these young people, as they approach adolescence, begin smoking themselves.

A major influence on children is a smoking parent. In a 1978–79 survey conducted for General Mills, 80 percent of parents interviewed said they felt they should set an example for their children in health matters. Yet when it came to smoking only 16 percent of the smokers among them had quit. Studies show that the children of smoking parents experience a gradual shift in attitudes as they approach adolescence. They become less concerned, and a number of them do start smoking.

When even one parent smokes, the teenager is more likely to smoke than if neither parent smokes. If an older brother or sister as well as both parents smoke, the chances are four times higher that the teenager will smoke than if there were no smokers in the family.

Whether parents approve of the teenager's smoking or not does not seem to matter. Both smoking and nonsmoking teenagers report that their parents do not—or would not—approve of their smoking. Even teenage smokers themselves say they hope their own children will not smoke. But the example of smoking parents or siblings apparently speaks louder than words.

Teenagers usually give peer pressure, not family influence, as the main reason they smoke. Almost 90 percent of teenage smokers report that at least one of their four best friends is a regular smoker. On the other hand, only 30 percent of nonsmoking students say the same. Among 3,000 junior high school students surveyed, having friends who smoked was found to be the most consistent predictor that a youngster would smoke.

Fourteen-year-old Sandy Rogers, a high school student in New York City, started smoking in the seventh grade. "I tried it and I liked it. All my friends did it," she said. Her friend, Francisco Hernandez, a seventeen-year-old, says he started smoking around the same time. He says he doesn't worry about the health issues. "These days you can get cancer from everything," he says. "The air that we breathe has chemicals in it."

The figures show a particularly alarming increase in smoking among teenage girls over the past twenty-five years. Experts say the rise has to do with changes in the sex roles of women. "It is a shame young women are falling into a trap as part of their goal toward equality with boys," said Irving Rimer, a spokesman for the American Cancer Society.

Because smoking is known to be risky, teenagers may seek to create the impression of flirting with danger. Some studies showed more smokers than nonsmokers also used marijuana, drank to get drunk, and believed in having fun now and forgetting about the future.

Since women began smoking decades after men, their smoking-related death and disease rates were not usually as high as the rates for men. In fact, the first Surgeon General's Report in 1964 barely touched on the problem of smoking among women.

But by 1979, the problem of smoking-caused illnesses in women was a major concern. The lung cancer rate for women had increased 500 percent.

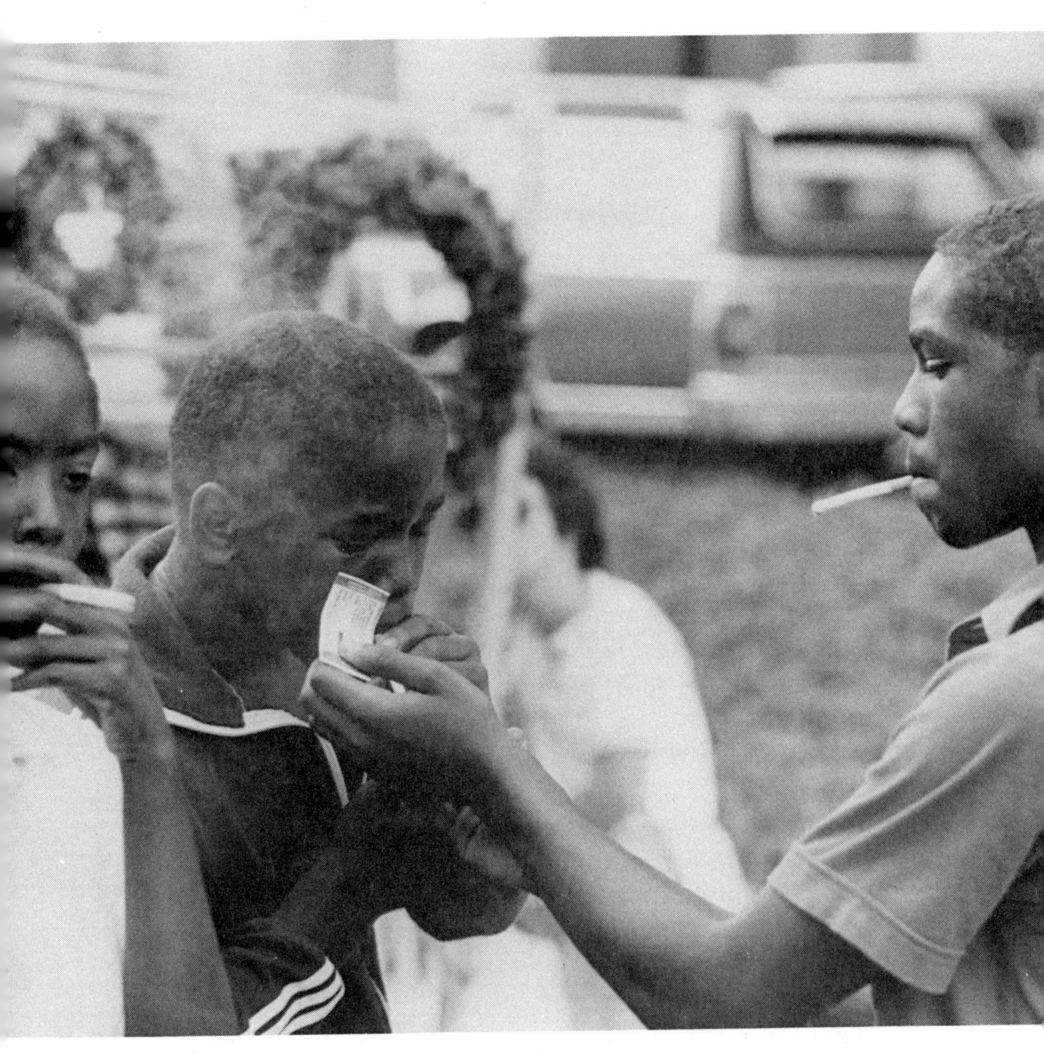

A group of teenagers smoking

Today, cigarettes have brought the age-adjusted death rates from lung cancer among women to even higher levels than the death rate from breast cancer.

The per capita consumption of cigarettes is now at its lowest level in years. But while the percentage of male smokers dropped from 42 percent in 1976 to 33 percent in 1985, there has been no similar sharp drop for females. In 1976, 32 percent of the women smoked; by 1985 the percentage had dropped to only 28. (One-third of all women who ever smoked have quit, however.) Many men are giving up cigarettes, and fewer boys are starting to smoke; but women apparently are reluctant to quit, and teenage girls are taking up the habit in increasing numbers.

Various national surveys have shown interesting relationships between smoking and other factors. For example, teenagers who have jobs are twice as likely to smoke as teenagers who are not employed. Also, students who plan to go to college are less likely to smoke than those who don't continue their education. One nationwide study on drug abuse suggests that smoking may be considered a first step toward the use of hard drugs and alcohol.

There also seems to be a connection between smoking and class status. "Smoking is slowly becoming a lower socio-economic problem," says John Pinney of Harvard University. In general, the average smoker is likely to have less money, be less well educated, and work at a less prestigious job than the average nonsmoker. Put another way, those who have higher positions in society tend to have lower smoking rates. Men who have higher incomes and college educations are less likely to smoke than those who have lower-paying jobs, are high school graduates, and do blue-collar work. The rate of smoking among black men is 10 percent higher than among white men.

Women tend to show exactly the reverse relationship. Women who work outside the home are more likely to smoke than housewives and women in households with low family income. White-collar workers are more likely to smoke than the blue-collar workers. Generally speaking, workers with the greatest exposure to industrial hazards have the highest rates of smoking.

A study by the federal Centers for Disease Control in 1985 shows that smoking generally declines with each level of education. More than 40 percent of white women who drop out of high school smoke, but only about 15 percent of white women with university graduate degrees have a smoking habit.

Researchers now think that fear and social pressure are having a limited effect in delaying the start of smoking. They are developing a number of different prevention programs that they hope will be more effective.

Educational Programs · In San Francisco, sixth-graders write essays about how cigarette advertising links smoking to images of beauty, sex appeal, and social success. In New York City, seventh- and eighth-graders practice refusing cigarettes from friends. In New Orleans, junior and senior high school students meet and talk with nonsmoking members of the Saints football team; school officials believe that professional athletes are good role models. All these schools, and many others across the country, share a common goal. They want to stop youngsters from smoking before they start.

Children get information that is too general and impersonal, says one teacher. As they get older they realize that people who smoke do not die instantly and that heart attacks or cancer do not always occur.

And since adolescents are mostly concerned with the here-and-now, not the future, they need more immediate evidence that smoking affects the body.

The new approach in prevention programs avoids the use of scare tactics related to the long-term dangers of smoking. "Kids . . . are concerned about what will happen to them now, not when they are seventy years old," says Joan Haskin, a health specialist. Therefore, smoking is presented to youngsters as a socially unacceptable behavior that has harmful immediate effects. Bad breath, smelly hair, and stained teeth and fingers are stressed. So is social rejection by nonsmoking friends and classmates and a loss in sports abilities.

School counselors give teenagers ways to say no to the various social urges to smoke. As an example, experts find that a smoking friend will back down when a nonsmoker says, "If you were a true friend you would not pressure me to do something I don't want to do."

Different techniques of antismoking education are also being explored for groups of varying ages and backgrounds. For instance, kindergartners may best learn that tobacco is harmful to them through the use of visual aids. Junior high school students, though, might interview family members to find out whether the adults who smoke regret smoking and what, if anything, they have done to stop. Pupils in senior high school can discuss the current controversy over the rights of smokers versus the rights of nonsmokers.

One prevention program that is being watched very closely is taking place in Sweden. There, a twenty-five-year effort is underway to make those born in 1975 a nonsmoking generation. A massive program of antismoking education is in full swing. At the same time, government controls over advertising and marketing of tobacco products are being expanded.

The Role of Advertising · The influence of ads on smoking behavior is difficult to measure. But it seems likely that teenagers are more affected than older groups. In a way, the young-looking models in the ads represent what every teenager wants to become. The underlying message of the ads is: if you smoke you'll be beautiful, happy, rich, and popular, with lots of fun-loving friends. For teenagers who are eager to be accepted as adults, the image is particularly alluring.

From the earliest days of cigarettes, the tobacco companies have spent increasingly large sums associating cigarettes with the trends of the times. Some of the first advertising efforts consisted of inserting a so-called cigarette card in each pack. These cards had pictures of battle scenes, Indians, baseball players, politicians, and so on. As time went on, pictures of movie stars appeared, too, and women in scanty costumes. To boost sales, one cigarette manufacturer even placed dollar bills in a few, randomly selected cigarette packs.

By the 1960s, tobacco companies were among the biggest advertisers on radio and television, as well as in newspapers and magazines, on outdoor billboards, posters on buses, subways, train stations, airports, taxis, and wherever else they could go to get their message across to large numbers of people.

But then, in 1964, the surgeon general's "Smoking and Health" report stated that, "cigarette smoking is causally related to lung cancer. . . ." One result was that, starting on January 1, 1966, all cigarette packs had to bear the message, "Caution—Cigarette smoking may be hazardous to your health."

The surgeon general's conclusion also resulted in the Federal Trade Commission's (FTC) taking a closer look at cigarette advertising late in the same year. This led to a number of voluntary announcements by the tobacco industry, which promised to avoid making

The world's first Tobacco advertisement

(Published in *New York City*
MAY 27, 1789)

True in 1789
true today

"*Best quality & flavor ... warranted as good as any on the continent ... will be sold reasonable!*" Those are the promises that Peter Lorillard made to tobacco buyers in 1789. And, today, they still hold good for another fine Lorillard tobacco ... Union Leader Smoking Tobacco.

If you marvel that a pipe tobacco so rich in flavor, so fragrant, and so mild costs only a dime...just remember that Lorillard's experience of a century and three-quarters goes into the selection and mellowing of Union Leader's choice Kentucky Burley.

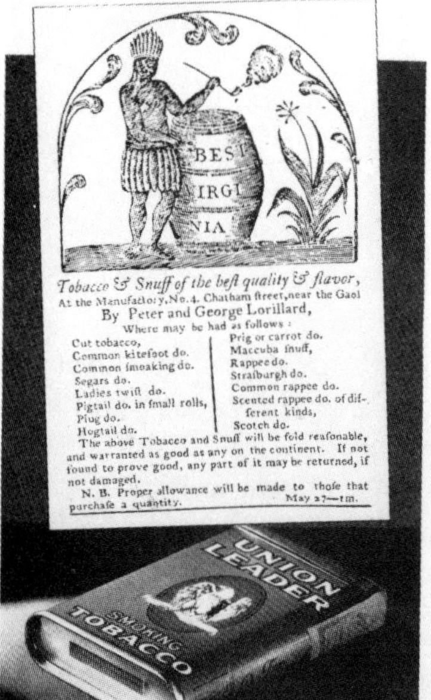

UNION LEADER

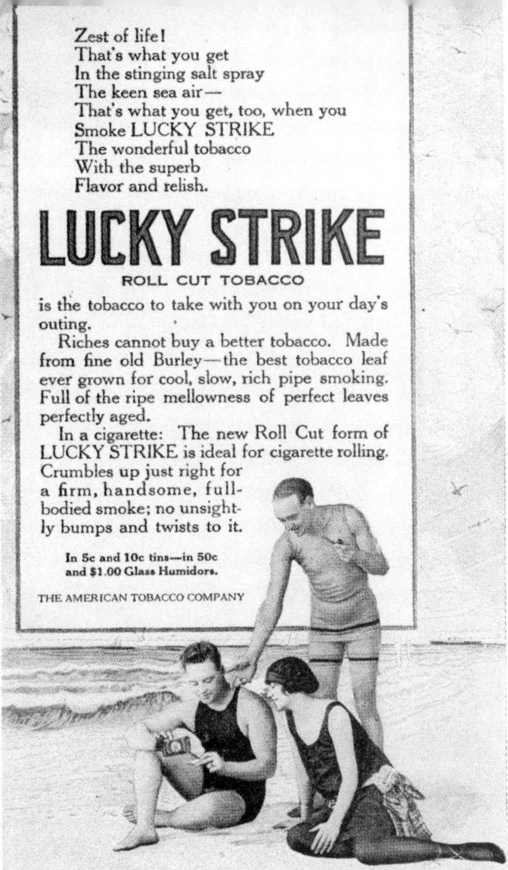

Several early advertisements inviting consumers to smoke. Cigarette advertising has been criticized for creating glamorous and sophisticated images of smokers

claims in ads that smoking is healthful. No ads would be placed in comic books or would appear on children's TV programs. Sometime later, tobacco advertisers also agreed to stop advertising in college magazines and on college campuses.

In 1966, John Banzhaf III, a Washington lawyer, challenged the broadcasting media. He asked for an opportunity to respond to the claims made in cigarette commercials, but all of the stations involved refused to grant him equal time. So Banzhaf appealed to the Federal Communications Commission (FCC), the government agency that supervises the broadcast industry. Even though the FCC also turned down his request, saying it just was not practical, they did apply their so-called Fairness Doctrine in 1967. The doctrine required broadcasters to provide free time for the presentation of antismoking advertising.

Starting in 1967, the American Cancer Society called for a complete ban on all cigarette advertising. One year later, the American College of Physicians spoke up for the ban of all cigarette ads on TV. On April 1, 1970, the warning label on cigarettes was changed to read: "Warning: The Surgeon General Has Determined That Cigarette Smoking Is Dangerous to Your Health." By the start of the next year, on January 1, 1971, the FCC finally banned all cigarette advertising on the public airwaves.

From the time of the Fairness Doctrine (1967) to the complete ban (1971), there was a sharp downturn in cigarette sales in the United States. An estimated 10 million Americans stopped smoking. Some say the decline was the result of the presence of the antismoking ads on television.

The radio and TV ban on cigarette ads, however, put a stop to the antismoking messages as well. Cigarette consumption began to go up again. Some think the ban may have indirectly helped to increase the sale of cigarettes!

The cigarette companies also found new ways to get mentioned on radio and TV. One method was to sponsor major tennis tournaments, auto races, bowling championships, jazz festivals, and horse races. Although no specific sales pitches were allowed, the names of the sponsors were shown again and again. And without the huge expense of the very costly radio and TV advertising, the cigarette manufacturers were able to spend even more money on other forms of advertising.

It is estimated, for example, that the cigarette companies doubled their magazine advertising budget and that the money they spent on newspaper ads went up nearly ten times! Currently, over $2 billion a year is spent on cigarette advertising. Of this total amount, about $375 million goes to magazine ads, $204 million is spent on newspaper ads, and $211 million is spent on outdoor billboard advertising.

Some newspapers and magazines refuse tobacco advertising for ethical reasons. The *Christian Science Monitor*, among some other newspapers, does not carry cigarette ads. Neither do certain national magazines, including *Good Housekeeping*, *Reader's Digest*, *National Geographic*, *Scientific American*, *The New Yorker*, and *Seventeen*.

The Controversy Over Cigarette Advertising · During the summer of 1986 the congressional subcommittee on Health and the Environment held two hearings on legislation to ban all forms of tobacco advertising. Those who favored the bill argued that cigarettes were a proven health risk. Continued advertising would encourage young people to start smoking, increase consumption among present smokers, lead former smokers to smoke again, and make it harder for them to quit.

Dr. C. Everett Koop, the surgeon general of the United States, stood up on behalf of the bill. Speaking for himself he said, "I'm a health officer, and anything that can lessen disability, disease, and death, I'm in favor of."

Opposed to the bill, as expected, were the tobacco industry and representatives of the advertising industry. All feared huge monetary losses if the ban on cigarette advertising became law. A ban would be ineffective, they said, and would harm consumers. Besides, they said, cigarette ads were aimed not at encouraging smoking but at influencing brand choice among habitual smokers.

Some civil libertarians joined the opposition and testified that the ban would be contrary to the Constitution. They held that censoring the ads of the tobacco industry would encourage the suppression of free speech. Instead, they advocate more government funding for antismoking literature and ads, and they support the warning labels on cigarettes.

The ban, according to the testimony of Barry W. Lynn, legislative counsel to the American Civil Liberties Union (ACLU), is both "unwise and unconstitutional." He says cigarette ads, which are legally classified as "commercial speech," are protected under the First Amendment if they

    concern a lawful activity
    are not misleading
    deal with a topic of substantial government
      interest.

The first point he explains this way. Smoking is clearly a lawful activity, even though most states prohibit the sale of cigarettes to minors and smoking in some public places. Since everyone is entitled to smoke, it is therefore wrong to deny the public information about tobacco products.

The second point is that although some cigarette

ads may be misleading, anyone can file a complaint with the FTC to order the removal of such misleading claims. Lynn disputes the claim of antismokers that all cigarette ads "deceptively portray the use of tobacco as socially acceptable and healthful."

Lastly, writes the ACLU spokesman, the ads deal with a matter that affects the health of its population. That is indeed a "substantial government interest." But even if it is in the interest of government to *discourage* smoking, Lynn feels that Congress must act within the limits of the First Amendment: "Congress may insist upon more speech designed to ensure that individuals are in a position to make an informed choice about whether to smoke. Congress may regulate the availability of cigarettes . . . and may place geographical limitations on smoking. Finally, Congress may seek to ban smoking altogether."

However, neither Lynn nor the ACLU believes that a ban on cigarette advertising would advance the government's interest. The net effect of advertising on the public's health may be overestimated. Many millions of Americans, says Lynn, see the cigarette ads but are not tempted to smoke. And there is little evidence that banning them would actually stop individuals from smoking.

The proposed ban on sponsorship of athletic or musical events and presentation of certain facts and opinions, he believes, may indeed go too far. Some cigarette ads, he points out, discuss the low tar or nicotine in a particular brand or even encourage smokers to be considerate of nonsmokers. Speech of such a factual or political nature is prohibited by the First Amendment. In addition, prohibiting sponsorship of major events by tobacco companies might represent a real loss for the public.

Several proposed bans on cigarette advertising are presently before the Congress. Representative

Mike Synar of Oklahoma has introduced a bill barring all cigarette advertising and promotion. Senator Bill Bradley of New Jersey and Representative Fortney H. Stark of California have offered a proposal to end the tax deductions for tobacco advertising and promotion.

Two other proposals are being considered. One would limit tobacco ads to what is called a "tombstone" format. The ads could give the name of the product and show the package but not have any other art or text. The other idea is to have an antismoking ad for every tobacco industry ad. The details of who would prepare these ads and pay for them have not been worked out.

Recently, the R. J. Reynolds Tobacco Company and the FTC were involved in a court case over a cigarette ad that disputed the research findings of a National Institutes of Health (NIH) ten-year study of smoking and heart disease. The FTC charged the tobacco company with "false or misleading" advertising on June 16, 1986.

The NIH research project, which was called the Multiple Risk Factor Intervention Trial (MR FIT), had followed 12,000 men who were at risk for heart disease because they smoked, had high blood pressure, and had high cholesterol levels. Half the men were given special diets, were treated for the high blood pressure, and were counseled to stop smoking. The other half received ordinary medical care. At the end of the ten years the number of deaths from heart disease was about the same in the two groups. But the death rate for men who had stopped smoking was 50 percent lower than for those who had continued smoking.

The R. J. Reynolds Tobacco Company ad said that the research showed that there was no proof that any of the factors being studied caused heart disease. It went on to say that linking smoking to heart disease "is an opinion. A judgment. But no scientific fact." It concluded by saying that "the controversy over smoking and health remains an open one."

The government questioned the following claims in the ad:

1. That the research was "designed and performed to test whether cigarette smoking causes coronary heart disease."

2. That the research showed that smoking was "not as hazardous as the public or the reader has been led to believe."

3. That the research "tends to refute the theory that smoking causes coronary heart disease."

At the hearing before Judge Montgomery K. Hyun the FTC argued that Reynolds had not accurately reported the research findings and had not mentioned the lower death rate among the men who had stopped smoking.

Floyd Abrams, the lawyer for Reynolds, said that the ad was an expression of opinion. As such, it was protected by the First Amendment. No government agency can regulate discussion about matters of public concern nor can it forbid expressions of opinion. Any person or agency that disagrees with Reynolds should refute the claims, but they should not try to silence the company.

Judge Hyun handed down his ruling on August 6, 1986. His decision went against the FTC; the complaint was dismissed. In his opinion Judge Hyun quoted Supreme Court Justice Oliver Wendell Holmes: "The best test of truth is the power of the thought to get itself accepted in the competition of the market."

Despite Reynolds' victory in court, however, the struggle to influence the public's attitudes on smoking goes on.

NINE

THE ECONOMIC ASPECTS

An applicant for a job as housekeeper at a Dallas hotel was asked whether she had smoked in the last six months. Since her answer was yes, she was not even considered for the job. By hiring only nonsmoking employees and accepting only nonsmoking guests, the employer says he saves thousands of dollars each year.

The figures support this hotel owner's position. Absentee rates for employees who smoke are approximately 50 percent higher than for nonsmokers. Smokers cost employers hundreds of dollars a year more in insurance claims than nonsmokers. In addition, in a hotel with only nonsmoking guests, the rooms can be cleaned faster, they do not have to be painted as often, and the insurance costs are lower.

But those who believe individuals should be free to smoke have a different viewpoint. They stress the economic contributions made by smokers and the tobacco industry, including the taxes paid and the jobs provided in growing, curing, manufacturing, transporting, and selling tobacco and tobacco products.

Costs to the Nation · Smoking is a factor in 90 percent of all lung cancer cases and about 30 percent of all cases of heart disease. These are both serious illnesses that require expensive medical treatment and hospitalization. It is estimated that our nation spends about $22 billion annually in caring for those sick with ailments brought on by smoking.

Gerry Oster, a medical economist, concluded that intensive care for underweight babies born to mothers who smoked during pregnancy costs Americans $152 million a year in medical expenses. He determined that maternal smoking was responsible for 5 percent of the nation's total annual cost of newborn intensive care. The care of these babies averaged $170 more than that of infants whose mothers did not smoke.

But the health costs of smoking are only about a third of the total national cost of smoking. The much greater cost is the lost productivity at work caused by smoking. These costs come about because smokers miss more days of work than do nonsmokers. Smokers also lose time on the job lighting up and smoking. And to this must be added the costs of air conditioning, ventilating, and cleaning the areas in which they smoke; the increased danger of fire; the higher fire and health insurance rates required; and the potential damage to expensive equipment, machines, and furnishings by cigarette smoke and ashes. Smokers also tend to die younger than nonsmokers. Each year almost 350,000 Americans die at an earlier age than expected because they smoked. Taken all together, smoking adds a whopping $43 billion a year to the costs of doing business in America!

Both the $22 billion in medical charges and $43 billion in loss of productivity are costs borne by every taxpayer in the nation. Tax money pays for public hospitals and the costs of training doctors. And higher prices for products and services cover the extra costs incurred by the employment of workers who smoke.

Costs to Business · Business managers are gradually accepting evidence which shows that hiring only non-smokers results in higher profits. One of the chief proofs comes from the surgeon general's health report of 1979. Males who smoke two or more packs of cigarettes a day miss 84 percent more days of work than nonsmokers. "Smoking is bad for the employees and the corporation," says Dr. J. Michael McGinnis of the federal Department of Health and Human Services.

The May 1981 issue of *Personnel Management* says that smokers add 10 percent in salaries, 30 percent in health and fire insurance premiums, 50 percent in equipment and furniture depreciation, 50 percent in cleaning costs, and 75 percent in disability and health benefits to the costs of a nonsmoker. On an individual basis, W. L. Weis wrote in the February 7, 1983, issue of *Business Week*, every year it costs $5,000 per smoker to cover the increased absenteeism and health care costs, lowered productivity, faster depreciation of furniture and equipment, higher cleaning and maintenance costs, and larger air conditioning and energy bills. The average cigarette smoker, for example, takes 30 minutes a day for lighting up and smoking activities; the average pipe smoker "wastes" fifty-five minutes daily in this way.

The Provident Indemnity Life Insurance Company now offers nonsmoking employees $300 discounts on health and life insurance premiums. The Aetna Life and Casualty Company offers 10 percent discounts to nonsmokers. And Blue Cross and Blue Shield plans in several states to offer discounts as high as 22 percent for subscribers who do not smoke.

The business world's growing sensitivity to smoking may spring from the current national passion for fitness and health, but more likely, it has to do with bottom-line profit. Business executives have learned that they can save money by hiring nonsmokers.

The U.S. Supreme Court recently ruled that it is not discriminatory to hire nonsmokers over smokers. This fact, though, is not widely known. A study, described in the July 1984 issue of *Management World*, found that 77 percent of those hiring college graduates to work in their businesses were not aware of the ruling. Thirty-seven percent, though, said that they already unofficially favored nonsmokers in their hiring practices.

Cost to Smokers · Smoking has been called "Public Health Enemy No. 1." But smoking is different from other environmental hazards. It cannot be curbed through the usual public health measures and massive expenditures of public and private funds. Basically, it is an individual habit that calls for individual action, a change in behavior.

As stated earlier, 90 percent of all cases of lung cancer are caused by smoking. About three-fourths of patients with his disease have the type called *non-small cell cancer*. Of these, some 20 percent undergo operations to remove the cancerous parts of the lungs. Where surgery is not possible, the cancer is treated with radiation therapy.

The rest of the patients have so-called *small cell lung cancer*. These patients are usually given a combination of powerful drugs, which is at least partially successful in most cases.

The Third National Cancer Survey (1974) showed the average hospital costs, at an average daily cost, (at that time, $274) for lung cancer patients, based on how long they survived after the onset of the disease:

Survival	Hospital Days	Total Cost
0– 6 months	30.5	$ 8,357
7–12 months	46.8	12,823
13–18 months	57.0	15,618
19–24 months	53.9	14,769

Abt Associates in 1980 studied the average *non-hospital* costs for a lung cancer patient who survived for one year. The figure they came up with included doctors' and nurses' bills, drugs, physical therapy, and so on. The total was $11,431.

In the book *The Economic Costs of Smoking and Benefits of Quitting*, the authors estimate the total costs of lung cancer by age of onset and sex. These figures, which include both the direct medical costs and the loss of productivity, further illustrate the staggering loss for victims of cigarette-caused lung cancer.

Age	Men	Women
30–34	$515,488	$248,944
35–39	458,052	219,624
40–44	384,800	188,348
45–49	304,421	155,228
50–54	219,927	121,785
55–59	139,159	89,599
60–64	72,371	63,350

The symptoms of heart disease associated with cigarette smoking range from intense chest pain (angina pectoris) to a heart attack (myocardial infarction) to sudden death. The usual treatment is a period of hospitalization followed by a course of drug therapy and a change in eating and exercise patterns to strengthen the heart.

The 1980 average first-year costs for someone suffering a heart attack were:

Ambulance and Emergency Room	$ 245
Hospital Charges	6,842
Follow-up Care	172
Total	$7,259

The figures for the total cost for patients suffering a heart attack by age and sex were as follows:

Age	Men	Women
35–39	$217,705	$131,155
40–44	174,853	111,150
45–49	130,210	90,272
50–54	87,495	69,365
55–59	61,743	50,036
60–64	32,290	34,609

As for respiratory diseases, the third major type of illness to strike smokers, the Office of Smoking and Health estimates that the risk of developing such conditions as bronchitis or emphysema is up to twenty times greater for smokers. About three-fourths of all respiratory-disease deaths are associated with smoking.

There is no cure for these lung-related conditions, which usually grow worse with time. In the early stages, a number of drugs can be used to relieve the symptoms of the disease. But as time passes, the drugs offer less and less help, and often the patient is either bedridden or hospitalized.

The direct medical costs of respiratory disease, year by year, from the onset are shown below. The total includes 1980 hospital charges, nursing home costs, physician fees, and drugs.

Year of Condition	Total Cost
1	$ 278
2	418
3	558
4	698
5	838
6	1,008
7	1,147
8	1,287
9	1,427
10	1,566
11	1,706
12	1,834
13	1,974
14	2,114
15	2,254
16	2,394
17	2,534
18	2,674
19	2,813
20	2,953

The total costs of lung disease by age and sex were:

Age	Men	Women
35–39	$405,207	$191,522
40–44	31,491	160,139
45–49	50,737	127,564
50–54	169,348	94,446
55–59	94,098	64,697
60–64	41,199	41,165

In addition to the health damage from cigarette smoking, someone who smokes spends a lot of money on the habit. A one-pack-a-day smoker forks over about

$500 a year on cigarettes. A person with a two-pack-a-day habit, of course, spends twice as much. According to the December 1983 issue of the *New York State Journal of Medicine*, Americans spend about $25 billion a year on cigarettes and other tobacco products.

Economic Benefits of Smoking · Tobacco growers and cigarette manufacturers are constantly criticized because they deal with a product believed by most to cause many serious, often fatal, diseases. But neither group shows any sign of abandoning its stake in the cigarette industry. Both consistently maintain, among other things, that tobacco sales are good for the economy.

Dr. Kenneth E. Warner in the December 1983 *New York State Journal of Medicine* estimates that the tobacco industry, from the farmer growing the leaf to the consumer smoking the cigarette, adds about $60 billion to the economy in this country. Nationwide, the tobacco industry employs over 100,000 farmers full-time and provides another 400,000 part-time jobs. The tobacco harvest generated over $1 billion in 1983 for North Carolina farmers and about $800 million for Kentucky farmers, according to the Department of Agriculture. Despite all the work required to plant, cultivate, and harvest an acre of tobacco (250 hours, compared to 3 hours for wheat), farmers are devoted to tobacco for one main reason: tobacco pays the bills.

The *New York State Journal of Medicine* and the Tobacco Institute both agree that all together the tobacco industry employs about 2 million workers. The tobacco industry accounts for roughly 2.5 percent of the gross national product (GNP), which is the annual total of all the goods and services produced in this country. And, according to the November 1985 issue of *Scientific American*, it contributes nearly $10 billion in federal, state, and local taxes.

Although the tobacco industry does pay many taxes, tobacco farmers also receive loans and subsidies from several federal programs. The Department of Agriculture runs a loan program to guarantee the tobacco farmer a fixed and high support price. If the farmer's tobacco crop cannot be sold on the market at the fixed price, a federally supervised corporation buys the tobacco with funds borrowed from the government. The corporation stores the tobacco crop and hopes it will be able to sell it later at a higher price.

Supporters of the loan program say that ending it would mean the elimination of many small farmers because the price they get for their tobacco would be too low to live on. Bigger farmers, they believe, would take over. The North Carolina Council of Churches issued a paper noting that disrupting the state's tobacco industry would "bring economic hardship, if not ruin, to a large number of its citizens." One tobacco farmer asked, "If you stop tobacco, what is going to happen to the people who maintain a livelihood on it?"

Critics of tobacco price supports, on the other hand, say that they should be ended because they work against the government's own findings on the health hazards of tobacco. Tobacco farmers, they add, should be encouraged to go into some other line of work, with government help if necessary.

But there are other issues that relate to the tobacco industry's "contribution" to the economy. A. E. Wood-

*Above: a tobacco seed-
ling being planted.
Below: tobacco puller
with freshly picked
tobacco leaves*

field, in the January 15, 1985, *Canadian Medical Association Journal*, says that an economy functions by providing goods that people want. Ignoring the smokers' desire to smoke cigarettes is unfair to consumers. According to Woodfield, it is also wrong to consider the medical costs related to smoking a drain on the economy. He believes that money spent on the smokers' doctors' bills actually benefit the economy—at least the medical industry.

Woodfield also points out that, on average, smokers die younger than nonsmokers. Premature death from smoking, he argues, represents a major savings in health costs, pensions, and retirement monies paid out to older men and women. The fact is that the Social Security System pays each smoker a total of $35,000 less than it pays each nonsmoker.

Taxes on Tobacco · Throughout history tobacco has been heavily taxed. The taxes are used, on the one hand, to raise money for government. Part of this money is also being used for purposes that range from providing health care for people suffering from smoking-caused disease to funding advertising campaigns to discourage smoking.

The other purpose of taxes is to discourage smoking. The demand for cigarettes is very much dependent on price. Economist Kenneth Warner has measured what he calls the "elasticity" of cigarette demand. According to his calculations, for every 10 percent increase in price, adults will smoke 4 percent fewer cigarettes. The influence is even greater on teenagers. Young men and women show a 14 percent decrease in smoking for every 10 percent increase in cost.

Federal excise taxes were first imposed on cigarettes during the Civil War. For the following century they were periodically raised. Then, with the enactment of the Tax Equity and Fiscal Responsibility Act of 1982 (TEFRA), the tax was set at 16 cents per pack. This provides the federal government with about $5 billion in revenue every year.

In addition, every state also has a cigarette tax. At this time, state taxes vary from 2 cents per pack (North Carolina and Oregon) to 26 cents per pack (Connecticut and Massachusetts). In 1985 taxes provided about $4 billion to the individual states, which is about 2.5 percent of the total taxes that the states collect. Although the money is added to the states' general funds, it is used mostly for education or cancer research.

Finally, cigarettes are considered a taxable item under the sales tax laws in a majority of states. When combined, these taxes are between one-fourth to over half of the average retail price of cigarettes.

Some people question the tax on cigarettes. They say it is a way that the majority, not liking cigarettes, imposes its will on those who smoke. The purpose of taxes is to raise money to run the government, in their view. Taxes are not to impose social values or to control the behavior of the citizens.

Excise taxes, these people say, cost the society dearly. As taxes go up, consumers buy fewer packs of cigarettes. The fall in cigarette sales cuts back production and leads to worker layoffs. A drop in the price of the tobacco leaf forces more farmers out of business, depressing the economy in the tobacco-growing states and adding to the welfare rolls.

Those who favor the taxes argue that smokers cost the government and nation money in additional health care and lower productivity. The higher taxes paid by smokers merely compensate the government for the extra expenses and loss of income that smoking incurs on the society at large.

Even as the large tobacco companies are advancing arguments on their economic "contributions," they are responding to the tide of antismoking reaction in the country. To protect their income during these years of controversy and to prepare for the possibility of a complete ban on cigarettes, they are expanding into other businesses. For example, Philip Morris now owns Miller Brewing Company, Seven-Up, and General Foods; R. J. Reynolds owns Kentucky Fried Chicken, Canada Dry, and Nabisco; and Brown and Williamson owns the department stores Marshall Field and Saks Fifth Avenue.

With control of these businesses comes more economic clout for the tobacco companies. One small example was reported in the *New York Times* on May 18, 1986. When Philip Morris took over General Foods, all posted signs urging employees to quit smoking were removed. But even more, those who deal with tobacco-owned businesses are reluctant to speak out or take any action against smoking that might antagonize the tobacco company and result in a loss of income.

The economics of smoking is a big issue before the American people. A significant point of the whole controversy hinges on the question of how bans on cigarettes or cigarette ads, changes in the tobacco tax, or changes in the price support system for tobacco farmers will affect the economic stability of our country.

TEN

THE LEGAL ASPECTS

Around the turn of the century, attorney Sam Scoville had this to say about spitting tobacco juice: "Every man has the inalienable right to spit on his own domain. In fact, the right to expectoration seems to be as constitutional in America . . . as the right to life, liberty, and the pursuit of happiness. If, however, by exercising this right a citizen spreads disease and death, or encourages others to do so, he should be impelled to forego this American birthright."

Remarkably enough, these words are still as pertinent to today's legal controversy over smoking as they were nearly a century ago. The essence of the current conflict is between the nonsmoker's right to breathe clean air and the smoker's freedom to smoke. The antismoking groups insist that the right to pure air has to take precedence. The prosmoking forces say that bans or restrictions on smoking are illegal—an infringement of constitutional rights.

Right to Clean Indoor Air · Historically, laws that limited smoking in public places were enacted principally for safety reasons. A majority of the states first prohibited smoking in order to protect the public against fire dangers, such as forest fires, gas explosions, and hotel fires. Restrictions were also placed on cigarette use in restaurant kitchens to assure that the food being prepared was not contaminated with cigarette smoke.

In the 1970s, scientists became more aware of the dangers of passive or involuntary smoking. Tobacco smoke emitted into the air of enclosed, indoor spaces, they found, could cause the same diseases as smoking itself. Since then a number of clean indoor air laws have been passed. They were designed to protect nonsmokers from being forced to breathe in second-hand smoke in public places. The term "public place" usually includes stores, factories, restaurants, schools, libraries, museums, theaters, sports arenas, waiting rooms, and planes, trains, and buses.

Minnesota was the first state to enact a statewide comprehensive law specially designed to protect nonsmokers from involuntary exposure to cigarette smoke. The Minnesota Clean Indoor Air Act (MCIAA) went into effect on August 1, 1975. The MCIAA protects the "public health and comfort and the environment by prohibiting smoking in public places and at public meetings, except in designated smoking areas." It was the first law to require separation of smokers and nonsmokers. The MCIAA has functioned as a standard or model that other states have followed when enacting similar laws.

Another especially important piece of clean indoor air legislation was the passage by the voters of San Francisco in 1984 of Proposition P, which is also known as the Smoking Pollution Control Ordinance. It followed by two years the recommendation of Surgeon General C. Everett Koop that nonsmokers avoid exposure to second-hand tobacco smoke whenever possible.

A smoker outside of an airport entrance. Airports are among a number of public places where smokers are prohibited from smoking except in designated areas.

A special feature of Proposition P was that it marked the first time employers were required to deal with nonsmokers' objections to smoke in the workplace. Employers must try to find solutions acceptable to nonsmokers. If that is impossible, smoking must be banned in that particular work area. Civil penalties are imposed on employers who fail to establish reasonable policies to protect nonsmokers. The acceptance of Proposition P marked the first major defeat for the tobacco industry, which had been opposing all laws regulating public smoking since the MCIAA was passed in 1975.

According to a 1986 survey by the American Lung Association, more than twenty states prohibit smoking in public buildings, restaurants, retail stores, offices, and other places where people work. At least twenty-seven states also limit smoking in schools and indoor cultural and recreational facilities. Some thirty states have long banned smoking on public trains and in health centers, except for in designated areas.

In addition to state regulations, the federal government has banned smoking, except in designated areas, in 6,800 of its office buildings across the country where 890,000 ptople work. The rules were issued by the General Services Administration and went into effect on February 5, 1987. The government hopes that the ban will encourage private industry to put similar policies into effect.

The need for laws to protect the health of nonsmokers rests on one undeniable fact: although it is possible to read alone or eat alone in a public space, it is not possible to smoke alone. Smokers can't prevent their tobacco smoke from pervading a room and nonsmokers can't stop breathing. Every nonsmoker who shares indoor air with a smoker is forced to become an involuntary smoker. If there are smokers present and there is no smoke-free area, the nonsmokers have no choice but to inhale the tobacco smoke, which is the same as making them smoke against their will.

Legislators recognize that most people work as a matter of economic necessity. One can choose to eat at home instead of going to a restaurant or can stay at home and watch television instead of going to a theater. But working for a living is not optional. Thus, protection from second-hand smoke in the workplace is of the utmost importance.

Voluntary restrictions on smoking in the workplace are not considered sufficient to protect the health of nonsmokers. Such controls have been compared with voluntary outdoor air pollution control measures. When left to themselves, polluters have not shown any great interest in checking the emission of hazardous substances into the atmosphere. For this reason, supporters of smoking bans have worked especially hard to obtain regulations on smoking in the workplace.

Smoking as a Public Nuisance · A public nuisance is defined as an act, or the omission of an act, that harms or annoys members of the public while going about their lawful activities. Only two states, Alaska and Arizona, have declared smoking a public nuisance. But the courts in any state can rule that smoking is a public nuisance, even if there is no specific public nuisance law on the books. Any individual who smokes in a public place and annoys others can be charged with creating a nuisance and be prohibited from smoking there.

This approach, however, has proved to be a rather ineffective way of controlling the problems of passive smoking. An individual, acting as a representative of the public, can sue only if he or she suffers "substantial" damages. (Being made uncomfortable by a bad odor, for example, is not considered substantial damage.) The courts have not yet decided if the irritation, discomfort, and possible health consequences of passive smoking are substantial enough to force those in charge of public places to prohibit smoking. Legal experts agree that a ban on smoking is better enforced if the owner of the public place—whether it be a restaurant, factory, store, or office—prohibits smoking on those specific premises.

Rights of Nonsmokers · In their book *The Legal Rights of Nonsmokers,* Alvan and Betty Brody insist that those who smoke in public places can be charged with assault and battery. Assault is the *threat* to use unlawful force or violence on a person. Battery is the *actual* use of force or violence. Such acts, though, must be intentional, illegal (see below) and offensive, to be considered assault and battery.

Anyone who lights a cigarette knows that it will create smoke that will go into the air. And, unless there is a wall separating smokers from nonsmokers, the nonsmokers will be forced to breathe that tobacco smoke. Therefore, it is intentional.

Studies have shown that the vast majority of nonsmokers do not want to be passive smokers and have not given permission to the smokers. Therefore, it is not permitted.

And finally, almost all nonsmokers find tobacco smoke irritating and annoying to breathe. Therefore, it is offensive. Following this line of reasoning, smoking in an enclosed space with a nonsmoker present can be considered assault and battery.

Some years ago a smoker refused to extinguish his cigarette when asked to do so by Dr. Joseph J. Kristan of Rockville, Connecticut. Dr. Kristan then aimed a spray of air freshener at the offending cigarette. He was arrested. By using the legal argument that he was defending himself against the smoker's assault and battery he was found not guilty.

Even though it may be legal to have a smoker arrested for assault and battery, taking every smoker to court is not very practical. But the fact that forcing others to breathe second-hand smoke is against the law establishes the principle that people have the right to be protected against involuntary smoking.

In Nebraska and Nevada, smoking is prohibited in public areas to protect public health and safety. California, among other states, has adopted a policy that recognizes the right of nonsmokers to a "smoke-free environment" in formal and informal meetings and in work stations. The law also holds that an employer is required to provide a safe workplace for his or her employees.

The rules about protection from exposure to dangerous tobacco smoke in the workplace were given a firm legal basis in 1976. Donna Shimp, who had worked for the New Jersey Bell Telephone Company for fifteen years, sued the company for not providing her with a healthful working environment. Allergic to cigarette smoke, Mrs. Shimp charged that the smoke in her work area caused her to suffer continuous irritation of her nose, throat, and eyes. In fact, she was made so ill that she had to stop working.

At the trial, Mrs. Shimp demonstrated that she had frequently requested either better ventilation or restricted smoking, but nothing was done. The judge ruled in her favor. He commented that the telephone company prohibited smoking near some of its sophisticated electronic equipment. "If such rules are established for machines," he said, "I see no reason why they should not be held in force for humans."

One far-reaching policy adopted by an employer is

that of Fortunoff's, a department store in Westbury, New York. That company decided three years ago not to hire smokers, even those who agreed not to smoke on the job.

Amy Lipson, a job applicant, challenged this non-smoking policy at a discrimination hearing. The department store's position was upheld. Fortunoff's senior vice-president for personnel, David A. Horn, defended the company position: "We're a health-oriented company and we're committed to preserving the health of our employees."

Smokers' Rights · The tobacco industry has spent millions of dollars to prove that the various bans in states, counties, and municipalities are "unnecessary and violations of personal freedoms." They claim that most bans are unfairly weighed in favor of non-smokers and discriminate against smokers.

Along with other critics of bans, they say that the ban violates, rather than protects, basic human rights. By spending public funds on convincing people not to smoke, the government neither allows free choice nor protects the right of smokers to smoke. Their position is that it is not a legitimate function of the state to forbid adults from doing something—like smoking—that is completely legal. And this applies even to actions the government judges to be harmful to the individual.

According to the smokers rights' argument, the nonsmoker has no more right to say that the air must be free of smoke than the smoker has the right to say it can be full of smoke. Both are owners of the same air. It might be argued that nonsmokers have a clear right to their lungs and what goes into them, even if they cannot control the air. But, of course, smokers have the same right. And since they share the same air, there is no simple way to resolve this conflict.

Given that one of the functions of government is to protect rights, it does not follow that the government need "do something" if being around smokers is either harmful or offensive. Even if a large percentage of the population disapproves of passive smoking, there is no specific requirement that a smoking ban should be made a public health policy. People should look to government last, not first, to reform behavior that some find objectionable. Any use of state power beyond the minimum necessary to guarantee peace and security for all individuals is destructive to society.

In a recent case, as in most previous private suits brought against the tobacco industry, the court ruled in favor of the companies that make cigarettes. In *Cippolone* v. *Liggett Group Inc.*, 1986, Rose Cippolone's husband claimed that the Liggett Group was liable for failing to warn of the hazards of cigarette smoking. In giving its decision the court said that the federally mandated health warning printed on cigarette packages protects the tobacco industry from failure-to-warn claims. To put it another way, the federal Cigarette Labelling and Advertising Act has precedence over state law claims that cigarette makers are liable for failing to warn of smoking dangers.

A number of business groups have come out against smoking bans and restrictions. Many restaurant owners, and managers, for example, feel that setting aside areas for nonsmoking is not only unrealistic but also burdensome and damaging to their business. "We continue to believe that mandated action, as opposed to a voluntary effort, is wrong," says Fred G. Sampson, president of the New York State Restaurant Association.

Referring to regulations to ban smoking in New York City taxicabs, George Babich, representing the Non-Medallion Taxi Association, says: "This type of legislation gives me the impression that our government thinks we're just plain stupid and can't manage our own personal lives. If our customers wish to smoke in our taxis, then let them smoke. Our customers are paying the fare, not the government.''

Other opponents express the view that there is no justification for prohibitions. The major problems include the fact that the government is curbing the liberties of citizens without proven need and that the government is violating the rights of citizens to hold and enjoy their private property.

They believe that it is the property owners and employers, not the state, who should decide the smoking policies in places they control. And patrons or workers should not complain because they knowingly accepted the conditions with respect to smoking when they entered the premises.

Another argument holds that the state should not ban smoking on government property because, technically, all citizens are equal co-owners. Imposing a ban is to discriminate against some of its owners. Further, it is wrong to assume that all *non*smokers are *anti*smokers.

Everyone agrees that the state has an obligation to prevent harmful behavior on government property. So, if exposure to second-hand smoke is in fact harmful, it could be banned from public places. But most of the prosmoking advocates consider the evidence for dangers of passive smoking to either be weak or nonexistent.

Still questioning the negative health effects of passive smoking, the antiban people advocate good manners and the forces of a free marketplace to solve conflicts between smokers and nonsmokers. Let employers and restaurant and office owners find the smoking policy that works best for them.

An antiban editorial in New York's *Daily News* on March 25, 1986, read: "Smokers and nonsmokers must work hard to understand and accommodate each other's needs, without government shoving them around—or creating laws that nobody could enforce." A few months later, the same newspaper repeated its opinion: "Smokers and nonsmokers *can* co-exist. It takes courtesy and mutual consideration. Draconian measures do nothing but build resentment and antagonism. There are *some* lessons to be learned from Prohibition. They [smokers] don't need strong-arm tactics. And as long as tobacco is legal, a politician's exercising the full power of the state—or city—against those who choose to smoke is, quite simply, arrogant and abusive."

A Last Word · A 1978 Roper Report prepared for the Tobacco Institute concluded that the nonsmokers' rights movement was "the most dangerous development to the viability of the tobacco industry that has yet occurred."

A 1985 survey showed that 75 percent of Americans felt smokers should not smoke in the presence of others, compared to only 69 percent who felt the same way in 1983. A report issued by the American Cancer Society in 1986 showed "vast social, cultural changes in smoking habits and attitudes over the past decade."

These reports tell us that the American public is increasingly turning against free, unrestricted smoking. Yet, some prosmoking groups, led by the tobacco industry, are still working very hard to turn back the clock. This controversy, which has been going on for about four centuries, will end only if we as a people accept the goal set by the surgeon general of making America smoke-free by the year 2000.

FOR FURTHER READING

Brody, Alvan, and Betty Brody. *The Legal Rights of Nonsmokers.* New York: Avon, 1977.

Brooks, Jerome E. *The Mighty Leaf.* London: Redman, 1953.

Diehl, Harold S., M.D. *Tobacco and Your Health: The Smoking Controversy.* New York: McGraw-Hill, 1969.

Henningfield, Jack E. *Nicotine.* New York: Chelsea House, 1985.

Oster, Gerry, Grahs A. Colditz, and Nancy L. Kelly. *The Economic Costs of Smoking and Benefits of Quitting.* Lexington, MA: Heath, 1984.

Shephard, Roy J. *The Risks of Passive Smoking.* London: Croom Helm, 1982.

Sobel, Robert. *They Satisfy: The Cigarette in American Life.* New York: Anchor, 1978.

Tollison, Robert D., ed. *Smoking and Society.* Lexington, MA: Heath, 1986.

Troyer, Ronald J., and Gerald E. Markle. *Cigarettes, The Battle Over Smoking.* New Brunswick, NJ: Rutgers University Press, 1983.

Winter, Ruth. *The Scientific Case Against Smoking.* New York: Crown, 1980.

Action on Smoking and Health (ASH)
2013 H Street, NW, Washington, DC 20006
202-659-4310

American Civil Liberties Union (ACLU)
132 West 43 Street, New York, NY 10036
212-944-9800

Group Against Smokers' Pollution (GASP)
P.O. Box 632, College Park, MD 20740
301-577-6427

Office on Smoking and Health
Park Building 1-58, Rockville, MD 20857
301-443-1690

Tri-Agency Tobacco Free Project
1575 Eye Street NW, Suite 1025, Washington, DC 20005
202-898-0580

The Tobacco Institute
1875 I Street, NW, Suite 800, Washington, DC 20006
202-457-4800

SOURCES

NEWSPAPERS AND MAGAZINES

Business Week
 "Office Smokers Feel the Heat," November 29, 1982
Daily News
 "Smoking Bill Clouds the Issue," March 25, 1986
New York Times
 "Surgeon General Warns on Snuff," March 26, 1986

 "Reynolds Faces F.T.C. Charges," June 16, 1986

 "Continuing Battle Over Tobacco," September 28, 1986

 "Plan to Restrict Smoking in New York City," April 13, 1986

 "Smoking Restrictions Growing in Workplace," June 19, 1986

 "Conflicting Views of City Smoking Bill," May 19, 1986
Time
 "A Cloudy Forecast for Smokers," April 7, 1986
Washington Post
 "The Wrong Way to Stop Smoking," July 18, 1986

PROFESSIONAL JOURNALS

American Journal of Public Health
"Is Smoker/Nonsmoker Segregation Effective?," July, 1982

American Lung Association Bulletin
"A Tale of Two Companies," May-June, 1983

British Medical Journal
"Nicotine . . . in Smokers and Nonsmokers," April 3, 1982
"Passive Smoking," June 2, 1984

Bulletin of the New York Academy of Medicine
"The Problem of Passive Smoking," December, 1981

Canadian Medical Association Journal
"Costs and Benefits of Cigarette Smoking," January 15, 1984
"Time for Action," November 1, 1982

Czechoslovak Medicine
"Chronic Bronchitis in Nonsmokers," 1980

Editorial Research Reports
"Tobacco Under Siege," October 5, 1984

Journal of Environmental Health
"The Implications of Sidestream Cigarette Smoke," November, 1978

Journal of Public Health Policy
"A Rebuttal to the Tobacco Industry," September, 1984

Journal of the American Medical Association
"Nonsmokers' Rights," May 19, 1978

Journal of the Iowa Medical Society
"On Tobacco Smoke and the Nonsmoker," March, 1978

Journal of the Israel Medical Association
"Passive Smoking," April 1, 1981

Lancet
"Smoking and Health," April 12, 1980

Management World
    "Giving Smokers Notice," July, 1984
New England Journal of Medicine
    "Cigarette Advertising," February 7, 1985
    "Smoking," August 22, 1985
New York State Journal of Medicine
    "The Economics of Smoking," December, 1983
    "An Indoor Air Quality Standard," July, 1985
Preventive Medicine
    "Passive Smoking," November, 1984
Psychological Reports
    "Effects of Tobacco Smoke in College Class-
        rooms," 1978
Supervisory Management
    "Cold-Shouldering the Smoker," September 3, 1981

In addition, see the books listed in the "For Further
Reading" section of this book.

INDEX